MAXnotes

Virgil's

Aeneid

Text by
Tonnvane Wiswell
(M.A. Arizona State University)

Illustrations by
Arnold Turovskiy

Research & Education Association

Dr. M. Fogiel, Director

MAXnotes® for
AENEID

Printed in the United States of America

Library of Congress Control Number 2001088473

International Standard Book Number 0-87891-001-8

MAXnotes® is a registered trademark of
Research & Education Association, Piscataway, New Jersey 08854

What MAXnotes® Will Do for You

This book is intended to help you absorb the essential contents and features of Virgil's *Aeneid* and to help you gain a thorough understanding of the work. Our book has been designed to do this more quickly and effectively than any other study guide.

For best results, this **MAXnotes** book should be used as a companion to the actual work, not instead of it. The interaction between the two will greatly benefit you.

To help you in your studies, this book presents the most up-to-date interpretations of every section of the actual work, followed by questions and fully explained answers that will enable you to analyze the material critically. The questions also will help you to test your understanding of the work and will prepare you for discussions and exams.

Meaningful illustrations are included to further enhance your understanding and enjoyment of the literary work. The illustrations are designed to place you into the mood and spirit of the work's settings.

The **MAXnotes** also include summaries, character lists, explanations of plot, and section-by-section analyses. A biography of the author and discussion of the work's historical context will help you put this literary piece into the proper framework of what is taking place.

The use of this study guide will save you the hours of preparation time that would ordinarily be required to arrive at a complete grasp of this work of literature. You will be well prepared for classroom discussions, homework, and exams. The guidelines that are included for writing papers and reports on various topics will prepare you for any added work that may be assigned.

The **MAXnotes** will take your grades "to the max."

Dr. Max Fogiel
Program Director

Contents

> **Each Book includes List of Characters, Summary,
> Analysis, Study Questions and Answers, and
> Suggested Essay Topics.**

MAXnotes® are simply the best – but don't just take our word for it...

"... I have told every bookstore in the area to carry your MAXnotes. They are the only notes I recommend to my students. There is no comparison between MAXnotes and all other notes ..."
– *High School Teacher & Reading Specialist,*
Arlington High School, Arlington, MA

"... I discovered the MAXnotes when a friend loaned me her copy of the *MAXnotes for Romeo and Juliet.* The book really helped me understand the story. Please send me a list of stores in my area that carry the MAXnotes. I would like to use more of them ..."
– *Student, San Marino, CA*

"... The two MAXnotes titles that I have used have been very, very useful in helping me understand the subject matter reviewed. Thank you for creating the MAXnotes series ..."
– *Student, Morrisville, PA*

A Glance at Some of the Characters

Aeneas

Venus

Dido

Deiphobe

Evander

Camilla

Pallas

Turnus

SECTION ONE

Introduction

The Life and Work of Virgil

Born in 70 B.C. Publius Vergilius Maro grew up in northern Italy on a gentleman's farm. His parents recognized his talents and gave him a good education, hoping he would take up a career in law. After studying in northern Italy at the schools of Cremona and Milan, he went to Rome in 53 B.C. to complete his training as a lawyer. Neither the city nor the occupation appealed to him, and after pleading his first case he returned permanently to the countryside.

From the Bay of Naples, Virgil (as he is called in English) began to write poetry. Ignoring the tide of chaos overwhelming Rome, he chose to focus on pastoral subjects. His first work, the *Eclogues* ("selections"), were presented as poems of shepherds. The descriptions of happy flocks and bucolic love were well received by the Roman public, who wanted to hide from the turmoil of their lives in poems that celebrated and romanticized the simple life. Two years later, in 42 B.C., Virgil found his estates confiscated by Julius Caesar's heir Octavius. Fortunately, his work had won for him the attention of Maecenas, Octavius's good friend and the premier literary patron of the time. With Maecenas' help, he had his farm restored to him.

Virgil's next work was the *Georgics*, a treatise on farming. Written over the course of seven years, it was finished in 31 B.C. In form it is a "how-to" book, but the lavish detail and beautiful verse turn it into a celebration of the importance of husbandry. While farming itself was in decline and most farmers were indifferent to the moral value of their occupation, city-dwellers once again found the work perfectly suited to their tastes.

With his reputation and finances secured, Virgil was able to devote the last 11 years of his life to the *Aeneid*. It was Augustus who suggested Virgil use the history of the Roman Empire as the subject for an epic poem. In it he attempted to take the works of Homer, who was considered the best of poets, and turn his words and style into a celebration of both the Roman nation and the Latin tongue.

While returning from a research trip to Greece, Virgil fell mortally ill. Unable to complete his work, he ordered it to be burned upon his death. Augustus countermanded Virgil's wishes, and he commissioned two of Virgil's fellow poets to edit the work. Upon its publication, the *Aeneid* was immediately hailed as a masterpiece and adopted as the official poem of Augustus' "Restored Republic." Since then, it has never fallen out of popularity.

Historical Background

Virgil lived through some of the most traumatic and glorious episodes of Roman history, as the democratic Roman Republic gave way to monarchic Imperial Rome. A decade before Virgil's birth, Sulla established a dictatorship, previously resorted to only in moments of crisis, as a long-term method of rule. The Republic was reinstated after Sulla's death, but the rise of murderous conspiracies, riots, and the use of private armies by battling factions made this form of government less viable.

The situation finally disintegrated into civil war in 50 B.C. as the two leading candidates fought for the position of chief of state. Caesar finally pushed his rival Pompey out of Italy in 49 B.C. He declared himself dictator, but was killed a few years later by men who wished to re-establish the Republic.

Their attempt failed and civil war ensued again. This time it was Caesar's adopted heir, Octavius, and Antony who fought for control of the empire. Antony was decisively defeated in the Battle of Actium in 31 B.C. Octavius returned to Rome not just as the victor in a civil war, but as a sovereign who had crushed a rebellion. His restrained rule, masked by the continued existence of the Senate, the Assembly, and important magistrates, provided the illusion that it was indeed a Restored Republic, as he preferred to call it. In 27 B.C., the same year he declared the Restoration of the Republic, Octavius added Augustus, "the holy one," to his name. Despite choosing this title for its non-monarchical ring, Caesar Augustus was actually Rome's first emperor.

The peace that Augustus' triumph brought to Rome gave a feeling of optimism to the Roman people. After the years of unease, it was time to celebrate life and the wonderful accomplishments of Rome. The end of civil war was a golden age for poets; there was time to reflect and write, and money was now available to spend supporting writers.

Given the mood, it is difficult to criticize Virgil's glorification of Augustus in the *Aeneid*. Virgil inserted several references to Augustus' incipient deification and provided "proof" of his supernatural ancestry. The institutions that Augustus wanted to strengthen were written into the *Aeneid*, giving them an air of sanctity appropriate for their ancient roots. Finally, the accomplishments of Augustus, "foretold" in the prophecies of the *Aeneid*, were established as the greatest accomplishment of the entire Roman race, achieved through centuries of suffering and sacrifice.

Yet, as David Slavit writes, Virgil's "celebration of the Roman past and present" is also "an implied demand upon [Augustus] and his heirs [to] live up to the poem's expectations and justify the epic sufferings [of its characters]" (Slavit, 89). There are indeed occasional intimations in the poem that Augustus' arrival may not have heralded the end of grief for the people of Rome. Virgil's pessimism proved to be well founded. The tragic death of Augustus' heir, Marcellus, led to Augustus being succeeded by an incompetent. He was followed in turn by Nero and Caligula, who abused the powers available to an absolute ruler, making it clear to all that there was indeed no more republic to be found in Rome. In the end, the lesson the *Aeneid* taught to Rome is that the gods have no interest in bringing about a happy ending, either for a magnificent city or its suffering people. The gods care only for themselves.

Virgil was fortunate enough to be a writer who was appreciated during his lifetime. The *Georgics* and *Eclogues* left him a rich man when he died. The *Aeneid* was immediately hailed as a masterpiece by critics and by the regime, and it was included as an official part of Augustus' celebrations of 17 B.C.

Simple pandering to the regime could have been enough for Virgil to have been praised by his peers, but his works had lasting popularity. By the fourth century A.D., enough critiques and ephemera existed of Virgil for Servius, an amateur scholar, to assemble a giant commentary on the *Aeneid*. Virgil's fame continued into the Christian era. Unlike many "pagan" writers, Virgil was adopted by the Catholic church, thanks to his apparent prophecy of the coming of Christ in the fourth *Eclogue*. Others have seen his "prophecy" as an optimistic hope for a good heir for Augustus.

With the decline of Latin as a topic of general study, the *Aeneid* has been read less, and the recent challenges as to which books constitute the classics has no doubt eroded Virgil's audience. Yet Virgil's lyrical style and his ambivalent message about the nature of life continue to earn the *Aeneid* its laurels as a masterpiece of literature. It is truly a classic.

Master List of Characters

Aeneas—*Protagonist, son of Venus, son-in-law of King Priam of Troy, future founder of Rome.*

Allecto—*One of the Furies. She inflames the Italians with the desire for war.*

Amata—*Latinus' wife. She wants Turnus to marry Lavinia.*

Anchises—*Aeneas' father.*

Ascanius Iulis—*Son of Aeneas by Creusa.*

Camilla—*A warrior maiden allied with Turnus. Beloved of Diana, she is a merciless killer.*

Deiphobe—*The Sibyl (priestess of Apollo and seer). She conducts Aeneas to the underworld.*

Dido—*Widowed queen of Carthage, fated to love Aeneas.*

Euryalus—*A handsome Trojan youth. He is caught and killed by Italians while attempting to deliver a message to Aeneas.*

Evander—*King of the Arcadians. He offers advice to Aeneas and sends his only son with him to fight.*

Juno—*Queen of the gods, enemy of the Trojans.*

Jupiter—*King of the gods, kindly disposed toward Aeneas. Also called Jove.*

Juturna—*Turnus' sister, goddess of pools and rivers. She tries unsuccessfully to save her brother from Aeneas.*

Latinus—*Aged king of Latium. He does not wish to war with the Trojans.*

Lavinia—*Daughter of Latinus. She is a prize to be won.*

Mezentius—*An Etruscan tyrant allied with Turnus. He fights valiantly despite his evil nature.*

Nisus—*Devoted friend of Euryalus. Dies trying to save Euryalus.*

Pallas—*Doomed son of King Evander. The sight of his sword belt inspires Aeneas to kill Turnus.*

Turnus—*King of the Rutulians, Lavinia's suitor, leader of Latium's defense. He wants to chase Aeneas out of Italy forever.*

Venus (Aphrodite)—*Goddess of love, Aeneas' mother and patron.*

Characters from the Illiad

Achilles—*The mightiest Greek warrior, leader of the Myrmidons.*

Agamemnon—*Leader of the Greek forces attacking Troy.*

Ajax—*A mighty Greek warrior.*

Andromache—*Widow of Hector. Now married to Helenus.*

Cassandra—*Priam's daughter. Although she predicted the fall of Troy, she was cursed to have her prophecies ignored.*

Creusa—*Daughter of King Priam and wife of Aeneas. She is lost leaving Troy and returns as a ghost to prophesy Aeneas' future.*

Deiphobus—*Son of Priam. After the death of both Hector and Paris, he became leader of the Trojan forces. For forcing Helen to marry him, he was betrayed by her to Menelaus. Aeneas meets him in the underworld.*

Hector—*Eldest son of Priam. He appears to Aeneas in a dream warning of Troy's fall.*

Hecuba—*Priam's wife.*

Helen—*The most beautiful woman in the world.*

Helenus—*Priam's son and prophet of Apollo. Weds Andromache. Provides advice for Aeneas.*

Menelaus—*Brother of Agamemnon and husband of Helen.*

Paris—*Son of Priam. He was chosen by the goddesses Juno, Minerva, and Venus to judge which of them was most beautiful.*

Priam—*King of Troy. He is killed in front of his family by Pyrrhus Neoptolemus.*

Pyrrhus Neoptolemus—*Son of Achilles. After the sack of Troy he took Andromache as his concubine and Helenus as a slave. He was killed by Agamemnon's son, Orestes.*

Ulysses (Odysseus)—*Wily Greek leader. Travelled for ten years after the sack of Troy.*

Other Characters

Aeolus—*King of the winds.*

Apollo—*God of the sun. He is on the Trojan's side, but rarely participates in the war.*

Charon—*Ferryman of the river Styx.*

Cybele—*The Trojan's mother goddess. She has her sacred pines transformed into sea-nymphs.*

Cupid—*Son of Venus, half-brother of Aeneas, and god of love. He poisons Dido with love for Aeneas.*

Diana—*Goddess of the hunt, Camilla's patron.*

Iris—*Juno's messenger. Appears many times.*

Mercury—*Messenger of the gods. Sent to Aeneas to tell him to leave Troy.*

Neptune—*God of the sea. Helps Aeneas by calming the waters.*

Opis—*A member of Diana's troop of maiden huntresses. She avenges Camilla's death.*

Tiberinus—*The god of the Tiber River. He helps both the Trojans and the Italians.*

Vulcan—*God of fire. He forges a suit of armor for Aeneas.*

Aeneidae and Allies

Acestes—*King of Sicily. Aids Aeneas on his travels.*

Achates—*Aeneas' constant companion.*

Arruns—*An Etruscan fighter. He kills Camilla.*

Cloanthus—*Trojan leader and captain of the* Scylla.

Dares—*A famed Trojan boxer.*

Entellus—*An aged Sicilian boxer.*

Gyas—*Trojan leader and captain of the ship* Chimerae.

Iapyx—*Aeneas' healer. He sees the sudden healing of Aeneas' wound as a divine sign.*

Ilioneus—*A Trojan elder who speaks when Aeneas is not available.*

Menoetes—*Trojan pilot of the* Chimerae.

Mnesthus—*Trojan leader and captain of the* Shark.

Nautes—*Trojan seer. He advises Aeneas to leave a colony on Sicily.*

Orodes—*A Trojan soldier.*

Palinarus—*A Trojan pilot. He is pulled into the sea by Sleep.*

Pandarus and Bitias—*Twin Trojan giants. They open the gate to the Trojan fortress.*

Pyrgo—*An aged Trojan matron. She encourages the women to burn the boats.*

Sergestus—*Trojan leader and captain of the* Centaur.

Tarchon—*Leader of the Etruscan Agyllans, ally of the Trojans.*

Latins and Allies

Drances—*An elderly Latin statesman who is opposed to Turnus.*

Lausus—*Son of Mezentius. He dies saving his father.*

Magus—*An Italian fighting for Turnus.*

Numanus—*Brother-in-law of Turnus, taunter of the Trojans.*

Tolumnius—*The Rutulians' auger. He incites the Latin forces to fight during a truce.*

Tyrrhus—*Latinus' shepherd. He leads the Latin farmers against the Trojans to avenge the death of his pet stag.*

Venulus—*An Italian messenger.*

Other Minor Characters

Achaemenides—*An abandoned member of Ulysses' crew found on the island of the cyclops.*

Androgeos—*Greek warrior whose armor disguises Coroebus.*

Anna—*Dido's sister and confidante.*

Celaeno—*Leader of the Harpies. She curses the Aeneidae for warring against her people.*

Cymodoce—*Chief of the nymphs formed from Aeneas' ships.*

Laocoon—*Trojan priest of Neptune, killed by snakes.*

Panthus—*Aged priest of Apollo. He brings the household gods to Aeneas as Troy falls.*

Polyphemus—*The cyclops blinded by Ulysses.*

Sinon—*Greek soldier captured by the Trojans. Convinces them to take the wooden horse into the city.*

Summary of the Poem

The *Aeneid* is an epic poem, detailing Aeneas' journey. The first six books of the *Aeneid,* recount the adventures of Aeneas, the future founder of Rome. The last six books tell of the settlement of the Trojans in Italy and the war with the Italians.

After the fall of Troy, a small group of refugees (the Aeneidae) escaped, and Aeneas became their leader. Several prophecies predicted that this group would settle in Italy and become ancestors of the Romans. The Aeneidae suffer many hardships; similar to those suffered by Odyseus (attacks by the Cyclops, Scylla and Charybdis.) After wandering for years, the Aeneidae arrived in Italy, settling in Latium. Before they were accepted, they had to fight a terrible war. After slaying Turnus, Aeneas is free to marry Lavinia, the princess of Latium.

Virgil begins the poem as Aeneas is sailing on the last leg of his predestined journey to Italy. Tremendous storms batter his ships and they take refuge on the nearest land. Aeneas hears that Queen Dido is constructing Carthage. The Queen falls in love with Aeneas and begs him to tell her the story of the fall of Troy.

Aeneas relates the tale at the request of the Queen. After the fall, the band of exiled men sailed to Delos where the oracle of Apollo predicted that they would found a great nation. He details his adventures up to the present time for the Queen. Dido and Aeneas' love is ill-fated. He must follow the destiny the Gods have made for him. When he leaves Dido commits suicide.

The ships finally arrive in Italy, near Cumae. Aeneas visits the temple of Apollo to consult a prophetess. She appears to him and tells Aeneas of the war he will fight and of his enemies. He asks to descend into Hades, where he meets his father, Anchises. Anchises shows Aeneas his future heirs and the heroes of Rome.

The Trojans continue on and settle in Latium. Aeneas realizes his prophecy has been fulfilled. A war breaks out and Aeneas is given magical armor by the Gods for protection. Turnus, the leader of Latium's defense, attacks the Trojan camp, and many lives are lost. Turnus announces that the husband of Lavinia will be determined by a duel between Aeneas and himself. Aeneas kills Turnus in battle. The prophecies of the gods have been fulfilled.

Estimated Reading Time

There are many translations of the *Aeneid*. Each book can be read in about an hour or two, with a range of approximately 12-24 hours for the whole work.

SECTION TWO

Aeneid

Book One

New Characters:

Aeneas: *leader of the fleet of exiled Trojans*

Juno: *queen of the gods, enemy of the Trojans*

Aeolus: *king of the winds*

Neptune: *god of the sea*

Venus: *goddess of love, Aeneas' mother and patron*

Jupiter: *king of the gods*

Achates: *Aeneas' constant companion*

Dido: *widowed queen of Carthage*

Ilioneus: *a Trojan elder*

Ascanius Iulis: *Aeneas' son*

Cupid: *god of love*

Summary

Juno, still furious at the Trojan refugees, has heard that their descendants are destined to destroy her favorite city, Carthage. She has kept the Trojans from Italy, their fated destination, for many years. Now she sets Aeolus to destroy the remnants of the Trojan fleet as they sail from Sicily.

The boats start to fall apart in the ensuing gale. Some are dashed against rocks, others are swept away from the fleet. In the midst of the storm, Aeneas regrets that he did not die defending Troy.

Neptune is angry at the winds for intruding on his kingdom and orders them to return to their home. After he calms the waters, the remaining ships quickly land on the shores of Libya. Aeneas kills seven deer for his comrades to eat, then gives an inspiring speech that belies his own worries. After eating, the men wonder what has become of their lost companions.

Meanwhile, Venus approaches Jupiter and asks what Aeneas has done to be kept away from Italy. She reminds him that he has sworn that the Trojans are to be the ancestors of the Romans, who will rule sea and land. Jupiter tells her not to fear. He prophesies that Aeneas will wage a great war in Italy, where he will find a home for his people. His son, Ascanius Iulis, will rule for 30 years, founding the city of Alba Longa. Three hundred years later, the twins Romulus and Remus will be born in Alba Longa. Romulus will found Rome, a city destined for greatness. Eventually, a Trojan Caesar named Julius, after Iulis, will extend Rome's empire over the world, bringing peace with him.

Jupiter then sends Mercury to Carthage to make sure the Trojans are welcomed there. Dido, queen of Carthage, is inspired to treat the Trojans with kindness.

The next morning Aeneas, accompanied by Achates, reconnoiters the territory on which he and his fleet have landed. Venus appears to them in the guise of a maiden huntress. Realizing she is a goddess, Aeneas asks her what country he is in. She tells him he is within the territory of Queen Dido, who fled Phoenicia with the wealth of her murdered husband and founded a tiny kingdom in the land of the Libyans. She bids him to seek the palace of the queen, where he will find many of his lost companions. After briefly appearing as herself, Venus departs, leaving Aeneas and Achates veiled in a fog of invisibility.

From atop a hill, Aeneas and Achates are amazed by the sight of the construction of Carthage. They enter the city unseen and walk to the temple that Dido is constructing for Juno. Aeneas is saddened by the memories raised by the temple's depictions of the Trojan War.

Queen Dido, goddess-like in her beauty, enters the shrine and takes her seat on a throne. She is approached by several of the Trojans that Aeneas had believed were lost at sea. Ilioneus approaches her and asks that the Trojans be given permission to land and repair their ships. Dido promises to help them, even offering to let the Trojans settle in Carthage, where she promises they will be well treated.

Suddenly the fog dissipates, and Aeneas reveals himself to the queen. Dido welcomes him and his companions and prepares a feast. Aeneas requests that his son, Ascanius, return from camp with presents for the queen.

Anxious to ensure Aeneas' fortune, Venus sends her son Cupid to take Ascanius' place. At the banquet, Cupid breathes a passion for Aeneas into Dido. Dido then invites Aeneas to tell the gathering about the fall of Troy and his wanderings in the seven years that have passed.

Analysis

With its stirring opening, "I sing of arms and a man," Virgil introduces the main elements of the *Aeneid*: the story of Aeneas, refugee from Troy and mythical ancestor of the Romans, whose fate pushes him toward Italy; and war, the force which caused Aeneas' departure from Troy and which will later cause him to resettle his people in Italy. As a synecdoche, "arms" is used to mean "war," but armor will also play a significant role in the book, especially the armor forged for Aeneas by Vulcan.

Virgil chooses to open the *Aeneid* in the middle of the action ("*in media res*"), as is traditional for an epic poem. This device plunges the reader into an exciting episode, drawing one into the story with little explanation. A Roman reader would naturally be familiar with Homer's *Illiad* and *Odyssey*, as well as the various legends of Aeneas. For this reason, Virgil has little need to introduce his characters or provide detailed explanations of such things as the origin of Juno's wrath.

The story of the romance between Aeneas and Dido, however, is wholly of Virgil's invention (although he borrows the tale from Appolonius' *Jason and Medea*). Appropriately, Dido receives more of an introduction, with Venus telling her history and the narrative

describing her appearance and personality. She is compared to the goddess Diana and is shown to be a kind and wise ruler.

Although she seems the perfect match for Aeneas, there is little doubt as to her fate. Jupiter tells Venus that Aeneas must leave Carthage in order to found Rome. The Roman reader, familiar with the history of the Punic Wars (264-146 B.C.), would also know that Rome and Carthage were destined to become enemies, so any romance between two characters representing these cities would be star-crossed from the start.

The inevitably poor outcome of Dido's passion is also heavily foreshadowed in the text. For example, she is referred to as "luckless/Dido—doomed to face catastrophe" (993-994). The love Cupid gives her is "a poison" (962) which Venus wishes to use to "inflame the queen to madness" (921-922). More subtly, the inclusion of the Amazon queen Penthesilea among the scenes of the Trojan War depicted in Juno's temple presages Dido's fate. As explained by William S. Anderson, the queens initially contrast: Penthesilea rages while Dido is rational. But by the end of her affair, Dido will have lost all of her restraint, dying as tragically as did the Amazon queen.

One of the main themes that runs through the *Aeneid* is the contrast between uncontrolled rage and rational order. Juno is constantly depicted as furious and out of control. Her anger makes her irrational, and the source of her anger (a wounded ego) is petty. Propriety serves as no limit; she is willing to bribe others (as she offers Deiopeia to Aeolus), and even use the minions of hell to give the tiny remnants of the Trojans trouble. Her rage is depicted as a fire, a traditional source of destruction. Virgil uses the analogy frequently to show the ill effects of unrestrained feelings.

Order is shown in Book One in two important episodes with accompanying similes. First, the depiction of the construction of Carthage is the epitome of a well-run society. The arts of architecture and political discourse co-exist; those who do not contribute are harangued to do their fair share. Virgil compares Carthage's residents to bees, the insects on which he lavished attention in the *Georgics*. Second, Neptune restores order to the sea after Juno's chaotic disruption of his realm. Virgil uses a noteworthy simile here: Neptune is likened to "a man remarkable for righteousness

and service" who calms a crowd "rocked by rebellion" (210-214). For the Roman reader who had lived through the decades of civil war that rocked the state before Augustus took control, the reference was obvious.

This book also introduces Virgil's favorite epithet for Aeneas: "pious Aeneas." Although Aeneas certainly worships the gods, "pious" has a different meaning in the Roman context than it does in English. For the Roman, a pious man was a man who did his duty. Not only did that mean doing his duty to the gods, which meant performing the proper sacrifices and ceremonies, but doing his duty for his country, which would most likely involve self-sacrifice of some sort. As Aeneas avoids taking the easy path in favor of following the instructions of the gods, his piety will become apparent.

Finally, it is interesting to note that the book opens with Aeneas in the depths of despair, his limbs "slack with chill." This is his lowest point of the book, from which there is only room for improvement. Not only must he come to believe in the predictions for his future, as Jupiter reveals to Venus, he must stop longing for Troy.

How is it, exactly, that Aeneas evolves? There is much debate over the precise nature of his change. While some say he moves from sympathetic human to perfect (and boring) demi-god, others say he descends, becoming the embodiment of fury by the book's close. It is up to each reader to weigh the evidence and decide which route Aeneas follows.

Study Questions

1. What three reasons does Virgil give for Juno's anger?

2. Where have the Trojans just left?

3. What is ironic about the incipient romance between Dido and Aeneas?

4. Why can Aeneas walk about Carthage unseen?

5. On which two occasions do references to hunting appear in this book?

6. What omen does Venus say predicts the safe arrival of

Aeneas' fleet?

7. Who killed Dido's husband?

8. What epithet is used most frequently to describe Aeneas?

9. Who does Jupiter list last as Aeneas' descendant?

10. How does Cupid sneak into Dido's arms?

Answers

1. Juno's anger arises because of the judgment of Paris, the Trojans' descent from an illegitimate son of Jupiter ("the breed she hated"--42), and the displacement of Hebe, Juno's daughter, by Ganymede, a Trojan prince, as cup bearer of the gods.

2. The Trojans have just left Sicily.

3. Dido and Aeneas' romance is ironic because of the bitter hatred that existed between Rome and Carthage for many years.

4. Aeneas is hidden by a fog of invisibility placed around him by Venus.

5. References to hunting appear in Aeneas' killing of the seven deer and in Venus' disguise as a huntress.

6. Venus says that the appearance of 12 swans predicts the arrival of Aeneas' lost ships.

7. Dido's husband was killed by her brother.

8. Aeneas is frequently called "pious Aeneas."

9. Caesar Augustus, Virgil's king, is the last person listed in Jupiter's recounting of Aeneas' glorious descendents.

10. Venus disguises Cupid as Aeneas' son, Ascanius Iulis, so he can sneak close to Dido.

Suggested Essay Topics

1. While the first six books of the *Aeneid* imitate in many ways Homer's *Odyssey*, Aeneas is a very different man from

Odysseus. What virtues does Aeneas possess? What methods does Virgil use to show Aeneas' character? If possible, contrast Aeneas to the Homeric hero.

2. The gods play an important role in the *Aeneid*. How does Virgil use them? Describe the roles played in Book One by Juno, Jupiter, and Venus, both as actors and as vehicles for manipulating the audience.

Book Two

New Characters:

Laocoon: *Trojan priest of Neptune*

Sinon: *Greek soldier captured by the Trojans*

Hector: *son of King Priam of Troy, recently deceased*

Panthus: *priest of Apollo*

Coroebus: *ally of King Priam*

Cassandra: *daughter of King Priam*

Androgeos: *Greek warrior*

Pyrrhus: *Greek warrior, son of Achilles*

Priam: *aged king of Troy*

Hecuba: *Priam's wife*

Summary

Aeneas begins the sad tale of the fall of Troy. After many years of war between the Greeks and the Trojans, the Greeks build a giant wooden horse. The Greek fleet sails out of sight, leaving behind the horse, which is filled with well-armed soldiers.

Although believing that the Greeks have left, the Trojans are unsure what to do with the horse, which they believe to be an offering to Minerva. The priest Laocoon has almost convinced the gathered crowd that the horse needs to be destroyed when a group of shepherds appears with the deceitful Greek soldier Sinon. Sinon tells the Trojans that he has run away from the Greek forces after being chosen as a human sacrifice. Then, pretending to break a vow of secrecy, he tells the Trojans that the horse is an offering to win Minerva's favor for the Greeks. However, he adds, it was prophesied that if the horse came within the walls of Troy that the Trojans would take over Greece.

Suddenly, a pair of giant snakes appear from the sea. They kill Laocoon and his two young sons, then slither to Minerva's temple. The Trojans take this as a sign to disbelieve Laocoon's warnings. They drag the horse toward Troy, where they break down the city walls in order to take the horse inside.

That night, the Greeks sail back to Troy. Sinon lets the warriors out of the wooden horse's belly. They open up the gates and let the other Greeks enter the unsuspecting city.

Meanwhile, Hector appears to Aeneas in a dream. He warns Aeneas that Troy is falling and tells him that he should take Troy's household gods to the city he will eventually found. Aeneas wakes up and is about to leave when Panthus arrives with the household gods. He tells Aeneas that the city is overrun. Aeneas nonetheless leaves to defend the city. He meets up with several Trojan men, who succeed in killing many Greeks by dressing in the armor of their victims. Coroebus, wearing Androgeos' armor, tries to save Cassandra and becomes the first of the group to die.

Aeneas runs into the palace, joining in its futile defense. Pyrrhus breaks down the palace doors. While Priam watches from the household altar, Pyrrhus kills Priam's son Polites. Priam attempts to fight, but Pyrrhus kills him also.

Aeneas briefly contemplates killing Helen, whom he sees hiding. Venus then appears to him and orders him to go to his family. She shows him that the fate of Troy was determined by the gods, not by Helen.

Back at home, Aeneas finds that his father, Anchises, refuses to leave. Just as Aeneas is about to return to the fray, a heavenly fire appears around the head of Ascanius. Anchises is swayed by this and the sight of a shooting star to leave Troy. Aeneas, leading Ascanius, carries his father out of the city on his back. In the chaos Creusa is separated from them.

Leaving his father at a shrine, Aeneas returns to the sacked

city to find Creusa. After much searching, he is met by her ghost, who tells him that he is to have another bride and a kingdom when he reaches the Tiber river. Aeneas finally returns to his father. He is surprised to find a large number of refugees assembled and waiting for him to lead them. As the sun rises, the group leaves for the mountains.

Analysis

In this book, Virgil displays his lyrical style through a series of similes that gives the events of the fall of Troy a heightened sense of tragedy. Aeneas, listening to the attack of the Greeks, is like a bewildered shepherd listening to a river tear apart cultivated fields (414-421); the women of the palace hide from the palace like doves driven by a storm (694-695); the city collapses like an ancient tree falling from a mountainside (845-853). The overall effect is of a natural disaster over which the human victims have no control. While these often lengthy similes are only one of the many stylistic elements Virgil uses in imitation of Homer, Virgil applies his sensitivity to the natural world (as developed in the *Georgics* and *Eclogues*) to put his own stamp on the technique.

Virgil is also a much more lyrical writer than Homer. Homer excelled in the description of battle scenes. In his other descriptions, he tends toward a realism that is at times so unheroic as to be humorous. Virgil, who never served as a soldier, writes woodenly of war. His excellence is in the romantic description of places that only exist in his imagination, such as the halls of the gods and the caves of the underworld.

Aeneas, as portrayed in Book Two, is initially the model of a Greek hero. He is determined to participate in a useless defense of Troy, not once thinking about saving himself. It takes three supernatural interventions and an appeal for him to think of his family before he is finally convinced to leave the city. At this point Aeneas' Roman virtues begin to appear: rationality and self-control are shown as he forsakes his opportunity to die a glorious death, filial duty and piety as he prioritizes saving his father and the household gods. His voyage toward his new home has often been interpreted as a personal transformation from a "barbaric" Greek into a "civilized" Roman.

From the death of Laocoon to the description of Pyrrhus, snakes play a strong symbolic role in this book. Slithering across the waves, Laocoon's killers' "blood-red crests" and "eyes drenched with blood and fire" foreshadow the destruction of Troy in flames (291, 296). Pyrrhus, "like a snake fed on poisonous plants," appears as a force of pure evil; he is indifferent to the blasphemous nature of the murders he commits. Deceitful Sinon is given a name that parallels the Latin word for coils (*sinus*, as in the English sinuous). The horse itself is said to slither its way up to the city. Overall, the motif of the snake reminds the reader of the deceit that has brought down Troy, adding a sense of horror to the pathos.

In this book the theme of the uncaring gods runs strongly. Neptune does nothing to save Laocoon, and Minerva chooses to destroy him for attempting to thwart her plans; the household gods turn their backs on Priam's family; Ripheus, the man who was "first among the Teucrians for justice and observing right," falls because the gods were indifferent to his virtue (573-575). Venus makes an appearance to save Aeneas, but her actions against Dido in the previous book show that she is as merciless as the rest of the Pantheon.

This theme fits in nicely with one of Virgil's personal inclinations—a hatred for war. Rather than glamorizing war, Virgil shows it to be a waste of lives and potential. For example, instead of talking of the eternal fame won by Aeneas' fighting companions, Virgil gives each of them a short description that creates a sense of tragedy at their deaths. Indeed, Virgil creates the feeling that anonymity after death seems to be the rule, rather than the exception—even for King Priam, whose body lies headless on the beach, "a corpse without a name" (750). In later books, Virgil vividly enumerates a variety of gory deaths met on the battlefield. Even the winners in the battles are not praised; they are depicted as slaughterers even when they are on "the right side." Virgil's underlying tone is one of pacifism.

A few elements of this book remain open to debate. First, why is it that Aeneas wonders why Hector appeared to him wounded? Every Trojan would have known of the mutilation of Hector's body as it was dragged behind Achilles' chariot. According to Patrick Kragelund, the traditional interpretation is that the dreaming

Aeneas had forgotten that Hector was dead. Drawing from Roman divination, Kragelund's interpretation is that Aeneas' understood Hector's wounds to be prophetic, but was unsure of what specific bad event they foretold. Hector's wounds symbolize the ruin of Troy.

A second questioned passage is Aeneas' encounter with Helen. For Aeneas to consider killing a defenseless woman is extremely unheroic, perhaps even out of character. The fact that the passage does not exist in some texts of the *Aeneid* has led to a debate over whether or not Virgil even wrote it. William Anderson, in *The Art of the Aeneid,* concludes that Virgil wrote it, but the people who edited the *Aeneid* after Virgil's death excised it. Whether or not Virgil would have included it, the scene casts a pallor on Aeneas' character that presages his later lack of compassion.

Study Questions

1. Who is the first to tell Aeneas of his future in Italy?

2. What two opinions exist concerning the nature of the Trojan horse?

3. What pastoral metaphor describes the Greeks' murderous entry of Priam's palace?

4. How does Sinon repay the kindness of the Trojans?

5. What do the Greek ships do while the Trojans debate over the nature of the horse?

6. What action of the murderous sea snakes convinces the Trojans that Minerva does not want them to harm the horse?

7. What double blasphemy does Pyrrhus commit?

8. Who is really to blame for Troy's fall?

9. What other names are used for Troy?

10. Why is Aeneas, the brave warrior, so nervous as he leaves Troy?

Answers

1. It is Hector who first tells Aeneas that he is destined to establish a great city.

2. While some Trojans believe the horse is a sacred offering to Minerva, others believe it is a Greek trick.

3. Aeneas says that a flooding river, dragging "flocks and folds across the fields," would be less furious than the slaughter of the Greek soldiers (668).

4. After being given refuge within Troy, Sinon opens up the Trojan horse, setting free the soldiers within it.

5. The Greek ships depart Troy's harbor, making it appear that they have returned to Greece.

6. The snakes take refuge in Minerva's temple after killing Laocoon.

7. Pyrrhus not only murders a son in front of his father, but also murders (twice) on a household altar.

8. It is the gods' restlessness that is responsible for Troy's downfall.

9. It is also called Ilium and Pergamus.

10. Aeneas, as he leaves Troy, is worried about the safety of his father and his son.

Suggested Essay Topics

1. While epithets are poetically necessary to fill out a meter, a good poet will use them to add to his work. What do Aeneas' epithets reveal about his personality and his destiny?

2. Examine the encounter of Aeneas and Helen. Why does he wish to kill her? How does this episode affect your interpretation of Aeneas' character? Would you exclude this passage from the *Aeneid*, and why?

Book Three

New Characters:

Polydorus: *murdered son of Priam*

Celaeno: *leader of the Harpies*

Helenus: *Priam's son*

Andromache: *Hector's widow, now married to Helenus*

Achaemenides: *an abandoned member of Ulysses' crew*

Palinarus: *a Trojan pilot*

Polyphemus: *the cyclops blinded by Ulysses*

Acestes: *king of Sicily*

Summary

The Trojan exiles build a fleet at the base of Mount Ida. When summer arrives, Anchises bids them to set sail. Their first settlement is in Thrace, which was formerly allied with Troy.

While tearing a myrtle branch from a nearby bush, Aeneas is dismayed to find blood dripping from it. A voice from the ground below announces that he is Polydorus, slain by the king of Thrace. He bids Aeneas leave this country. After holding a proper funeral ceremony for Polydorus, the Trojan exiles depart.

The Aeneidae (followers of Aeneas) land in Delos, home of the shrine of Apollo. Aeneas prays to Apollo for guidance. They are told to return to their ancient home. Anchises says that the oracle must return to Crete, ancestral home of the long-dead Trojan King Teucer.

The Trojans arrive in Crete and build a new home there. Not long after their arrival, a pestilence falls on the people and the crops. Before they can return to Delos for further advice, the household gods appear to Aeneas and tell him that he is supposed to go to Italy, birthplace of ancient King Dardanus of Troy.

En route to Italy, a storm washes the fleet upon the shores of the Strophades, home of the foul Harpies. Aeneas and some of his men kill some of the Harpies' goats and cattle. The Harpies contaminate their meal twice, and when the Trojans try to fight

the Harpies off they find they cannot hurt them. Celaeno curses them for stealing their animals and then attacking them, saying that the Aeneidae will not found their settlement in Italy until hunger has forced them to eat their tables. The Trojans leave and sail to Actium, where they spend a year.

The fleet then goes to Buthothrum, where they find Helenus has become king and taken Andromache as his wife. Aeneas first encounters Andromache, who is praying at the empty tomb of Hector. She tells Aeneas that she was Pyrrhus' concubine, but that Agamemnon's son Orestes had killed Pyrrhus, making Helenus heir to a small kingdom. Helenus then approaches and takes them into the city. He prophecies the route the Aeneidae will have to take to Italy, warning them to avoid Scylla and Charybdis and advising a visit to the Sibyl before the journey's end.

After reluctantly departing this friendly land, the Trojan exiles unknowingly come to the island of the Cyclops. After a frightening night, they encounter Achaemenides, who begs them for sanctuary. He warns them to quickly depart this land of man-eating monsters. Upon seeing the blinded Polyphemus the fleet quickly departs, barely escaping his clutches.

After more sailing, Aeneas' group docks in Drepanum, on the island of Sicily. There Anchises dies, and from there the Trojans came to Carthage. Aeneas at last ends his tale.

Analysis

Over the course of the third book, Aeneas experiences a quiet revolution. From being a man who follows his father's occasionally wrong advice, Aeneas becomes a man accustomed to leadership. His divine sanction as leader is confirmed in the vision of the household gods, which announces Aeneas' troop's destination to Aeneas—not his father. Roman society highly valued "patria potestas"—the power of the father. Had Anchises survived, Aeneas would have still been obliged to give him a leadership position. With Anchises gone, it is Aeneas who now leads, acquiring the epithet "Father Aeneas."

As Aeneas has now been repeatedly told of his destiny to found a city, he also becomes a man with a mission: to take his people not just to a new land, but to Italy. For this reason, despite the

many obstacles placed in his way, Aeneas continues to push on. The supernatural nature of the oracles he has received make it almost impossible for him to do otherwise. Indeed, settling in Italy becomes not just a goal; it becomes a duty that Aeneas must fulfill. This devotion to duty over personal pleasure is what makes Aeneas a true leader in the Roman vein.

Virgil's imitation of the *Odyssey* is apparent in Aeneas' visit to the island of the Cyclops where he meets a member of Ulysses' crew. Other similarities exist in Aeneas' near encounters with the enchantress Circe and the monsters Scylla and Charybdis. Like Ulysses, Aeneas will also visit the underworld in book six, which concludes the *Odyssey*-inspired half of the *Aeneid*. The second six books are often called the *Iliad* half, but they do not follow Homer's plot so closely. Instead, they incorporate lesser events of the Homeric epic while emulating the Homeric style.

After the high drama of the fall of Troy, Book Three provides a break in what has been a tense story line. This pattern of following a momentous book with a less dramatic one is one of the basic structural features of the *Aeneid*. Virgil's preference for variety is at odds with Homer's style. The difference can be explained by the contrast in Homer's and Virgil's intended audiences. Homer's repetitive style aided memorization and was appropriate for oral story telling. Virgil, however, wrote with the intent of being read. For this reason not only does he carefully organize the books into alternating patterns of action and relaxation, but Virgil also, according to R. D. Williams, "varies his accounts of landings and departures to avoid any repetition" (Williams, 43).

Study Questions

1. What curse does Celaeno cast on the Trojans?
2. What sign does Helenus say will show Aeneas where to found his city?
3. To whom does Helenus advise Aeneas to make sacrifices?
4. Why do the Trojans found a colony on Crete?
5. What religious practices are discussed in this book?
6. How was Polyphemus blinded?

7. What happens when Aeneas attempts to pull branches off the Thracian myrtle?

8. How did Andromache come to be married to Helenus?

9. Aside from Scylla and Charybdis, what must the Trojans avoid on their way to Italy?

10. Where does Helenus advise Aeneas to take no count of time during his visit?

Answers

1. Celaeno curses the Trojans to eat their plates before they find their new home.

2. Helenus tells Aeneas to look for a snow-white sow with 30 piglets.

3. Helenus advises Aeneas to make sacrifices to Juno.

4. Anchises, believing that King Teucer is the Trojan ancestor to whom the oracles refer, chooses Crete as the appropriate destination.

5. There are many religious practices in Book Three. For example, at the funeral for Polydorus, offerings are made of bowls of milk and blood; Aeneas pours wine on the hearth after the vision of the household gods; and following the advice of Helenus, the Trojans take up the practice of wearing a purple mantle on the head when they make sacrifices.

6. Polyphemus was blinded by Odysseus and his men.

7. The tree bleeds blood instead of sap.

8. After taking Andromache as a prize from Troy, Pyrrhus eventually married Hermione and gave Andromache to Helenus.

9. The Trojans must take care to avoid hostile Greek forces on their way to Italy.

10. Helenus advises Aeneas to spend as much time as necessary at the cave of the Sibyl.

1. As will be seen in Book Four, Aeneas' story has only made him more attractive to Dido. What elements of Aeneas' tale could she sympathize with? How has Aeneas been made to look great? What other portions of the tale could have drawn Dido closer to Aeneas? Draw from both Books Two and Three.

2. Analyzing the prophecies of Aeneas' future, show how they both predict and influence Aeneas' actions. Does Aeneas still have free will?

Book Four

New Characters:

Anna: *Dido's sister and confidante*

Mercury: *messenger of the gods*

Iris: *Juno's messenger*

Summary

Dido is now raging with love for Aeneas. She tells her sister Anna that Aeneas is the only man who has ever tempted her to break her vow to be faithful to the memory of her dead husband. Anna advises her to follow her feelings, inasmuch as the union between Aeneas and Dido would be good for the kingdom.

Dido's love begins to drive her mad. Without her attention, the construction of the city comes to a halt. Seeing Dido thus afflicted, Juno conspires with Venus to unite their favorites in marriage. Venus suspects Juno is only trying to save Carthage, but she agrees to help because it will help Aeneas.

The next day, Dido and Aeneas go on a hunt. A sudden, tremendous storm sends the pair into a cave for shelter where they copulate. Dido believes this to constitute a wedding between them, but the rumor spreads that she has given up properly ruling her city in favor of indulging herself in lust. This causes great consternation among the leaders who had vied for her hand.

When Jupiter hears of the couple's activities, he sends Mercury to tell Aeneas that his destiny is to be master of Italy, and he must set sail. Mercury goes to Carthage, reminding Aeneas that he must think of his son's future and stop wasting his time building a woman's city.

Terrified by Mercury's appearance, Aeneas tells his crewmen to equip the fleet in silence while he tries to approach Dido with the bad news. The rumor finds Dido before Aeneas does, and she attacks him for trying to sneak away. She begs him to take pity on her, in the name of their marriage and in light of her lost reputation. Denying that they have been married, Aeneas says that it is the god's will that he departs. Dido chastises him for his lack of sympathy, finally wishing him a lonely death. She faints and is carried away.

The Aeneidae quickly prepare their boats. Dido sends her sister to ask Aeneas to wait at least until the winds are favorable. Aeneas ignores Anna's pleas.

Dido is driven over the edge by Aeneas' incipient departure. She decides that she wants to die. She tells her sister to build a pyre and stack her bridal bed and Aeneas' armor on it, explaining that she intends to rid herself of her passion by burning his possessions. That night, while Dido tortures herself with thoughts of her misfortunes, Aeneas has a vision warning him to depart before something bad happens.

When Dido sees the empty harbor the next morning, she wishes she had set her forces upon Aeneas and destroyed him. She curses Aeneas to die early, without having enjoyed his new kingdom. She prays for an avenger to make the Trojan settlers suffer, damning the two kingdoms to eternal hatred. Dido then climbs the pyre and, after briefly reminding herself of what she accomplished before the curse of love befell her, plunges a sword in her heart.

Anna runs to her sister, who is dying a hard death. Juno sends Iris to set Dido's soul free. As Iris cuts a lock of Dido's hair, her life blows away.

Analysis

Although the reader has known from the start that Dido's love for Aeneas cannot survive, it is impossible not to feel pity for Dido. Like the Greek tragic heroes, her fall is terrible because she is initially so great. She has survived the treacherous murder of her husband and gone on to successfully lead her people to a new and prospering kingdom, an achievement so much more remarkable because of her gender.

Contrary to the Greek type of tragedy, it is not Dido's flaws that cause her destruction: it is a conspiracy against her by the unfeeling gods. Her initial love for Aeneas was planted in her through the deceit of Venus. The unhealthy nature of the goddess-given love is brought out in the narrative's reference to it as a "shaft of death" that is driving her to distraction (97). Hunting metaphors make Dido's victim status even more clear. Matched against a man who killed seven stags in a day, there is no resistance possible for this "heedless hind hit by an arrow" (92). For this reason, her removal from her city's business, though irresponsible, seems forgivable. Even her misguided marriage does not make her appear any lower in the readers eyes: how could a mere mortal resist the will of two goddesses?

Virgil uses a novel device to focus the reader's attention on Dido's agony. By keeping the narrative in the third person after his opening "I sing," his re-entry into the story at line 561 leaps off the page: "What were your feelings, Dido, then?" While doing little to develop sympathy for Aeneas, Virgil's question thrusts the reader into Dido's tortured mind. It is no wonder that, as noted in Slavit's *Virgil*, Dido was the first successful female character in Latin literature, eventually appearing as a heroine in the works of Chaucer, Marlowe, and the operas of Berlioz and Purcell. Despite being merely a footnote in Aeneas' movement to Rome, Dido carries her books well.

By contrast, Aeneas, although also a pawn of destiny, seems an unfeeling brute as he fails to respond to Dido's emotional pleas. Slavit, however, feels that Aeneas' "willingness to sacrifice comfort and safety and even, as far as we know, love for the abstraction of Rome's destiny is what makes him...annoying, but also...great" (Slavit, 117). Anderson adds that Dido, too, could have made better choices; for example, choosing to care for her kingdom instead of committing suicide. Yet given the nature of her

love for Aeneas, Dido seems to have few, if any, options. She has been crushed beneath the wheel of fate. To his advantage, Aeneas does at least try to say good-bye before he leaves; but in the face of the misery he causes, he looks like a cad. It is unsurprising that some have said that as Aeneas pursues his duty he loses his humanity.

Note how the gods take their own interpretation of events. Juno claims she wishes to work with Venus to seduce the two leaders in order to create an "everlasting peace" (132). Venus, however, believes that Juno merely wants the greatness that is supposed to come to Rome to befall Carthage. Nonetheless, she agrees to work with Juno. Both of their motives seem confused. Venus only cares for Aeneas' well-being, and while Juno claims to worry for Dido, her unwillingness to accept fate dooms the woman who is supposedly her favorite. Ultimately, each goddess is only concerned with how events on the mortal plane affect their own glory. Their removal from the human world makes both of them indifferent to the suffering they create.

Study Questions

1. To whom does Dido tell of her love for Aeneas?

2. What bad effects does Dido's passion have on her city?

3. Why do Juno and Venus cooperate to bring Dido and Aeneas together?

4. What simile describes Aeneas as he leaves the city to go hunting?

5. How is Jupiter alerted to Aeneas' dalliance?

6. How does Mercury insult Aeneas' efforts to build Carthage?

7. What does Dido say would confront her in the face of Aeneas' departure?

8. What differing views do Aeneas and Dido hold of their affair?

9. What curse does Dido wish upon Aeneas?

10. What service does Iris perform for Dido?

Answers

1. Dido tells her sister Anna about her feelings for Aeneas.

2. Dido's passion causes construction of Carthage to come to a halt.

3. Juno wants to make Carthage the great kingdom of the Mediterranean, while Venus wants to see her son succeed.

4. He is compared to graceful Apollo returning to Delos.

5. The prayers of King Jarbas alert Jupiter.

6. Mercury asks if Aeneas is a woman's servant.

7. Dido says she would be comforted if she were to have a child by him.

8. Dido sees it as a marriage, which Aeneas denies.

9. Dido wishes Aeneas to drown crying her name. She later curses him to watch as his people are slaughtered and be denied the enjoyment of his new kingdom, dying unburied in the sand.

10. Iris cuts a lock of hair from her head, enabling her soul to escape.

Suggested Essay Topics

1. There is much debate over Aeneas' "guilt" in the death of Dido. Is he responsible for her death? Toward whom is the reader's sympathy drawn?

2. Virgil is fond of the language of the hunt. Discuss the role of hunting in the *Aeneid.* How do the roles of hunter and hunted define the characters of Dido and Aeneas? Be sure to draw from Virgil's use of similes.

3. Dido comes to life brilliantly in this book, so much that she outshines Aeneas. Analyze the characterization of Dido, pointing out the many literary devices that Virgil uses to give her depth.

Book Five

New Characters:

Gyas: *captain of the ship* Chimerae

Menoetes: *pilot of the* Chimerae

Mnesthus: *captain of the* Shark

Cloanthus: *captain of the* Scylla

Sergestus: *captain of the* Centaur

Nisus: *devoted friend of Euryalus*

Euryalus: *a handsome Trojan youth*

Dares: *a famed Trojan boxer*

Entellus: *an aged Sicilian boxer*

Pyrgo: *eldest Trojan woman, former nurse of Priam's children*

Nautes: *Trojan seer*

Summary

From off the shores of Carthage, Aeneas sees a vast blaze. Although he does not know with certainty what is responsible for the fire, he knows that it is a bad omen because of Dido's extreme distress.

A great storm arises, forcing the fleet to land on Sicily instead of Italy. They are welcomed again by Acestes. By coincidence, they have arrived on the anniversary of Anchises' death. Aeneas decides to hold memorial sacrifices and athletic competitions in honor of his father. After making sacrifices to his father's shade, Aeneas announces that the games will be held ten days hence.

On the morning of the games, crowds gather on the beaches to watch. The first event is the boat race. Gyas, the initial leader, is unhappy with his pilot's refusal to sail closer to the rocks and throws the hapless Menoetes overboard, to the great amusement of the onlookers. Sergestus sails too close and catches his boat on the rocks. At the last minute Cloanthus offers a sacrifice to the sea gods if he wins. Portunus, god of harbors, hears him and pushes his boat ahead of Mnesthus. Everyone receives prizes, even Sergestus, who comes in last.

The next competition is a footrace. Nisus takes the lead, but slips in some blood left from the sacrifices. Nonetheless, he manages to trip Salius, who was behind him, letting his friend Euryalus win. Salius is angry at being cheated out of his prize, so he is given a consolation prize, as is Nisus.

In the boxing match that follows, Dares is about to take the prize uncontested when Aeneas rouses Entellus to have one last bout. Dares does better because of his youth, but Entellus has a sudden bout of pride after he is knocked down and begins to pummel Dares. Aeneas tears Entellus away and awards him the prize bullock, which Entellus kills with a well-placed punch as an offering to his teacher, Eryx.

The final event is a shooting match. Aeneas sets a dove up as a target. The third contestant manages to hit the dove, whose tether had been severed by the previous shot. King Acestes shoots an arrow just for the sake of show, but the shaft miraculously bursts into flame and disappears into the sky. Aeneas decides that this omen is a sign from the gods and awards Acestes the prize for first place.

As a conclusion to the games, the young Trojan boys parade on horseback. Meanwhile, Juno sends Iris to stir up the Trojan women, who are grumbling over still not having a home. Iris disguises herself as one of them and encourages the women to burn the boats. Pyrgo recognizes her as a goddess. The women do not act until they see Iris sail across the sky, whereupon they grab torches and set the boats aflame. Hearing of the fire, Aeneas rushes to the scene. Jupiter answers his prayers and sends a storm to quench the flames.

Discouraged, Aeneas contemplates settling in Sicily. Nautes recommends he leave behind those who are weary of travelling with King Acestes and then continue on to Italy. Aeneas is unsure what course of action to follow, but Anchises appears to him in a dream that night and tells him that Nautes' advise is sound. He further advises Aeneas to come visit him in Elysium, which he can reach with the help of the Sibyl. After spending a few days setting up the settlement and saying good-bye, the reduced band of Aeneidae depart.

Meanwhile, Venus asks Neptune to grant the Trojans a safe passage to Italy. Neptune says he will let them pass with only one life as payment. After a day of smooth sailing, all the sailors fall asleep except Palinarus. The god Sleep comes to him disguised as one of the Trojans and urges him to rest. After he refuses to abandon his post, Sleep drugs him and tosses him overboard. Aeneas is saddened when he awakes and realizes his old friend has been lost.

Analysis

The funeral games provide a light-hearted respite after the emotional drain of Book Four. Yet the games foreshadow sadder days to come. The humorous dunking of Menoetes is merely a prelude to the underhanded murder of Palinarus. Similarly, Nisus' devotion to Euryalus will come to a painful conclusion on the Italian battlefield. While the four games are united by sacrifices that bring success and the ethical treatment of victory in the battles to come, ethics will count for nothing and sacrifices will only bring more blood.

These games provide an excellent opportunity to see just how much Virgil has borrowed from the *Iliad*. In Homer's work, funeral games are held following the death of Patroclus. While Virgil added the boat race and eliminated some other sports, the events parallel those of the *Iliad*. For example, Homer's shooting contest has a dove whose cord is cut by a contestant's arrow, and his footrace has a contestant who slips and falls, although it is animal dung that causes him to lose his footing and not blood.

One of the modern major controversies over the *Aeneid* is whether or not Virgil is attempting to subvert the regime of Augustus. The historical opinion has always been that Virgil was supporting the regime with his work, as evidenced by Augustus' adoption of the *Aeneid*. This book provides proof of Virgil's direct support of the powers-that-be by his creating through the leaders of the Aeneidae, an ancestry for the modern Roman noble families. It is also possible that the very inclusion of this book was a bow to Augustus. The Romans did not care for these kinds of athletic contests; their idea of entertainment was gladiator contests and watching animals fight. Augustus had revived quadrennial sporting matches in 28 B.C. in honor of the victory at Actium. Virgil's inclusion of this book, which seems to have been added after most of the book was written, might be an attempt to encourage the practice. Augustus was also attempting to revive the Roman religion, and Virgil's inclusion of so many religious rites would make them appear more sacred and ancient in the eyes of his readers.

Finally, the curious flaming arrow seems to be a reference to Acestes' future as the founder of a great city, Acesta. As Segesta, this western Sicilian town was an important city in the first Punic War.

Study Questions

1. Why does Aeneas believe the sacrifice to his father's shade has been well-received?

2. What is symbolic about the prize Cloanthus receives?

3. To what is Sergestus' boat compared?

4. Why do the gloves of Eryx enable Entellus to kill an ox?

5. How does Pyrgo know that the disguised Iris is a goddess?

6. Who is it that actually hits the dove in the shooting match?

7. What are the Trojan women complaining about when Iris arrives?

8. What final, non-competitive event ends the day's festivities?

9. What "sacrifice" does Neptune want for providing the Trojans safe passage to Italy?

10. How does Palinarus fall into the ocean?

Answers

1. A snake slides from Anchises' funeral shrine and tastes all of the offerings.

2. The scene embroidered on the cloak is of Ganymede being snatched away by Jupiter's eagle. The replacement of Hebe by Ganymede as cupbearers of the gods is one of the reasons Juno cites for being angry with the Trojans.

3. His boat is compared to a wounded snake that still appears fierce despite having a broken back.

4. They have lead and iron sewn inside them.

5. Pyrgo has just spoken to the woman disguised as Iris.

6. Eurytion hits the dove.

7. The Trojan women are tired of sailing from place to place and want a city again.

8. An equestrian exhibit by the young men concludes the day's events.

9. Neptune wants just one human life in exchange for the safe passage he gives the Trojans.

10. After shaking a sleeping potion into his eyes, the god Sleep pushes Palinarus into the ocean.

Suggested Essay Topics

1. Carefully examine all of the prizes won during the games. Choose the three best and discuss their symbolism.

2. Examine the events of the boat race. How do the personalities of the captains reveal themselves in their sailing styles? What lesson can be learned from the results of the race? How do Roman values fit into the race's conclusion?

Book Six

New Characters:

Deiphobe: *the Sibyl (priestess of Apollo and seer)*

Charon: *ferryman of the river Styx*

Deiphobus: *the last leader of the Trojans after Paris' death*

Summary

The Trojans land in Cumae. Aeneas seeks out the cave of the Sibyl. He waits for her in the beautiful Temple of Apollo, which is beautifully carved with scenes from the life of Daedalus. The Sibyl orders Aeneas to make sacrifices, which he does. She is then possessed by Apollo, who predicts a great war in Italy and warns Aeneas of continuing harassment by Juno.

Aeneas then asks the Sibyl to lead him to the underworld (the "kingdom of Dis") so that he may visit his father. The Sibyl tells him that in order to enter, he must bring back a branch from the golden tree as an offering to Proserpina, Queen of the Underworld. She also orders him to bury Misenus, a recently dead companion. While chopping down trees for Misenus' tomb, Aeneas suddenly sees a pair of doves who lead him to the golden tree. He snaps off a bough and returns to the Sibyl.

After sacrificing many animals, Aeneas and the Sibyl enter the cave to the underworld. A variety of horrors lurk inside, such as Disease, War, and Strife. There is also a tree under which live savage monsters, such as centaurs, gorgons, and harpies. They terrify Aeneas, but with prodding from the Sibyl he passes them by.

When they arrive at the bank of the Styx, Aeneas is dismayed to see Charon turning down so many passengers. Among them he recognizes Palinarus, who says that he survived his fall into the ocean only to be killed by barbarians when he got to shore. The Sibyl tells Palinarus that there is no way he can cross the Styx until he is buried, but that a plague will fall on the guilty cities until they build him a tomb.

Charon lets Aeneas and the Sibyl enter his boat after seeing the golden bough. On the other side of the Styx, Deiphobe neutralizes Cerberus with a drugged cake. She and Aeneas cross different regions until they get to the Fields of Mourning. Aeneas sees Dido there. He begs her to speak with him, but she is silent and leaves him to return to Sychaeus.

In the land of the soldiers, Aeneas finds his brother-in-law Deiphobus, whose face has been disfigured. Deiphobus tells Aeneas the story of Helen's betrayal. Moving on, Aeneas is horrified to see the citadel of Tartarus. Deiphobe lists some of the legendary characters trapped within, then describes some of the punishments meted out within its walls.

Aeneas leaves the golden bough in front of a gate and enters the Groves of Blessedness in the Elysian Fields. He and the Sibyl find Anchises, who is overjoyed to see his son again. Aeneas is surprised

to see all of the souls waiting to drink from the river Lethe (forget-fulness) so that they may return to the mortal world.

Anchises finally reveals to Aeneas the fate that will await his descendents in Italy. He shows him his next son, who will be a king, and proceeds to Romulus, founder of Rome. He then points out Augustus Caesar. Anchises describes the sacrifices, patriotism, and courage of the various leaders of Rome, along with their great deeds. Ultimately, the Roman race will be one that teaches peace, humbles the proud, and spares the defeated.

Anchises fires Aeneas' soul with love of glory, then tells him of the coming battles in Italy. He then escorts Aeneas and the Sibyl to the two gates of sleep. After exiting through the gate of ivory, Aeneas hurriedly rejoins his ships.

Analysis

Book Six is the pivotal book of the *Aeneid*. Aeneas' journey to the underworld, a fantastic story in itself, provides the means for Aeneas to leave behind his past and work concretely toward his glorious future. Aeneas now knows that Dido's love is lost to him forever, and that he truly must seek the new wife Creusa predicted long ago. Deiphobus, with the disfiguration of the adulterer, serves as a subtle reminder of the sins of Troy that Aeneas has escaped and encourages Aeneas to accept his future as the source of glory for his dead Trojan friends. The slate has been wiped clean; there is no longer any reason for Aeneas to cling to the past.

After the frustrations Aeneas has experienced in his attempts to obey the will of the gods, Anchises at last gives Aeneas a clear vision of what he has been struggling toward. His speech, known as the Review of Heroes or Heroscopia, selectively examines Rome's history in order to provide the most positive vision of Aeneas' "future."

First, Anchises shows Aeneas the men who will found cities across Italy. Anchises reveals that Aeneas' descendents will eventually spread the power of Rome to the ends of the earth. To enable this to come to pass, Aeneas will have to found but one city. Second, Anchises' indication of Numa and Tullus, the priest "crowned with olive boughs" and the military leader who will "wake to arms the indolent," shows Aeneas the two paths *pietas* will oblige him to follow. He will continue to honor the gods, but he will very soon have to do his duty to his homeland as well. Finally, the continual references to heroes who have had to suffer personally in order to help the country show Aeneas that he is not alone. All of these men have had their eye on a higher good, and Aeneas can see that the suffering they (and he) undergo has been worth the price. After this great speech, it is no wonder Anchises addresses Aeneas as "Roman" (1135); Aeneas has finally transformed his allegiance to his future.

For the Roman reader, Virgil's choice of heroes and accompanying commentary would have had a varied result. First, the mention of Caesar and Pompey, whom Anchises urges to "not let such great wars be native to your minds, or turn your force against your homeland's vitals," would remind the reader of the recent, decimating civil wars which Augustus had finally brought to an end (1105-1106). If that were not enough to encourage loyalty to Augustus, Virgil's florid description of his god-surpassing attributes could inspire the reader to view Augustus' accomplishments with awe. In addition, Augustus' inclusion between the kings and the senators would show that he is a ruler who combines the best of both of the former rulers of Rome. Finally, Virgil's reminders of the sorrows necessary in moving Rome to its current state of excellence would inspire the reader with patriotism and a desire to serve the state well. Overall, the Review of Heroes would inspire loyalty in the citizens of Augustus' Restored Republic.

It is interesting to note Virgil's inclusion of a very public condolence in this section. The Marcellus upon whom Anchises wishes to scatter flowers was the nephew and designated heir of Augustus. His death in 23 B.C. meant the end of Augustus' dreams of establishing a dynasty and was considered a great tragedy.

Study Questions

1. How does Misenus die?

2. What birds are sacred to Venus?

3. To whom does Dido turn for comfort?

4. Why does Aeneas not attack the monsters within the cave

of hell?

5. What sort of activities do the dead enjoy in Elysium?

6. What similes does Virgil use to describe the gathering of the souls on the banks of the Lethe?

7. Who inhabit the Fields of Mourning?

8. What is symbolic about the father of Romulus?

9. What indicates that Numa is a priest?

10. What simile describes Dido's response to Aeneas' pleas?

Answers

1. He challenged Triton to a trumpeting duel and was dashed against the shoals for his insolence.

2. Doves are her sacred bird, and it is only fitting that they should show Aeneas the golden tree.

3. In death, Dido is comforted by the shade of her dead husband, Sychaeus.

4. The Sibyl warns Aeneas it would be useless, as the creatures do not have any substance.

5. In the Elysian fields the dead wrestle, they dance, they sing, and they care for their war horses.

6. He says they are like bees buzzing over a field of flowers.

7. The fields of mourning are inhabited by those who died for love.

8. The symbolism of having Mars as the father of Romulus (which was indeed the tradition) is that Rome was founded on war and the military virtues.

9. He is carrying offerings and is crowned with a wreath of olive leaves.

10. Dido is like "stubborn flint or some Marpessan crag" (619). The phrase echoes Aeneas' response to Dido's pleas in Book Four.

Suggested Essay Topics

1. What is the meaning of Aeneas' exit through the gate of ivory? What would it have meant if he had exited through the gate of horn?

2. How does this book serve as a pivot for the work? What expectations does the Heroscopia give the reader for the rest of the work?

Book Seven

New Characters:

Latinus: *aged king of Latium*

Lavinia: *daughter of Latinus*

Turnus: *king of the Rutulians, Lavinia's suitor*

Allecto: *one of the Furies*

Amata: *Latinus' wife*

Tyrrhus: *Latinus' shepherd*

Mezentius: *an Etruscan tyrant*

Camilla: *a warrior maiden*

Summary

After passing the island of Circe, the fleet of Aeneas sails up the Tiber River. In Laurentum, capitol of Latium, King Latinus is unsure of what to do with his only child, Lavinia. Although she is ready to be married, he has received strange signs about her future. The latest oracle had said that he must not marry Lavinia to a Latin, but to a foreigner. This is unfortunate, as Latinus' wife favored Turnus, the handsome Rutulian king.

On the shores of the river, the Trojans are having their first meal in Latium. Instead of consecrating the crusts of their bread to Ceres, they eat them along with their meals. Thus "eating their tables," they fulfill Celaeno's prophecy. The Aeneidae realize that at long last they are at their new home.

A.T.

The next day they scout the territory. While Aeneas plots out their new city, emissaries are sent to Latinus. Latinus welcomes the Trojans. Ilioneus says that they seek a small plot of land, adding that the gods told them to settle in Italy. After a pause, Latinus tells the Trojans that they must be the foreigners he was told to seek, and offers his daughter's hand to Aeneas. He gives them gifts and sends them back to the camp.

Juno is enraged that she has not yet managed to destroy the Trojans. She decides that even though Aeneas is fated to wed Lavinia, she can hold off the event for a time with a great and bloody war. Juno goes down to hell and asks the fury Allecto to cause a war.

Allecto quickly departs. She goes to Amata, who is already unhappy that her favorite is to be denied, and tosses a poisonous snake down her dress. As the venom works through her system, the queen becomes hysterical, eventually taking Lavinia into the forest and hiding her there.

Allecto then goes to the sleeping Turnus, appearing to him as an aged priestess of Juno. She tries to encourage Turnus to go to war for Lavinia. Turnus sneers at her and tells her to keep to women's work. Angered, Allecto appears as herself. She casts a torch at the terrified Turnus, who is filled with anger and the desire for war. He decides to drive the Trojans out of Italy.

Allecto finds Ascanius, who is out hunting. She puts the scent of a stag in the nose of his dogs and the love of praise in Ascanius. The deer which Ascanius shoots is unfortunately the pet of Tyrrhus. He and the farmers set off to punish Ascanius. Suddenly, the Trojan exiles and the Italians are at war.

Allecto returns to Juno, proud of her work. Juno is pleased and sends Allecto back to her cave. All of the Italians run to Latinus and ask him to declare war. He refuses, locking himself in the palace. Juno then bursts open the symbolic Gates of War.

After an invocation to the muse, Virgil gives the catalogue of Italian heroes, including their leaders and places of habitation. Most notable of the Italian forces are Turnus, Mezentius the tyrant, and Camilla, the warrior maiden.

Analysis

Despite the cheerful start this book has, Virgil has filled it with details that point to the coming war. First, Lavinia's episode with the heavenly fire mirrors the dream Paris' mother had of giving birth to a firebrand. Lavinia's flame indicates that she, too, will bring great trouble to her people, although, like the flame around Ascanius' head in Book Two, it also symbolizes that Lavinia will have great glory.

Second, and as discussed by Michael Putnam in *Virgil's Aeneid*, the "cluster of bees on Latinus' laurel is one harbinger of future domination by the Trojans" (Putnam, 13). Its symbolism is drawn from Virgil's discussion of bees in the fourth *Georgic*, where Virgil describes bees' war-like demeanor and their habit of swarming when they are looking for a new place to live.

In addition, Latinus' gifts to the Trojans cast an ominous shadow. While he welcomes them in peace, the presents he sends—a chariot and horses that breathe fire—are more appropriate for war. Finally, the red of the waters as Aeneas arrives at the Tiber hints that soon the river will run red with blood.

It seems odd for Virgil to spend so much time glorifying the Italian heroes, since they are the enemies of the book's protagonist. The inclusion of a list of Italian heroes has an important political implication. For most of its life, the Roman Republic had only granted citizenship to those who were of Roman ancestry. This left most Italians disenfranchised and highly dissatisfied. After the Marsic War, which lasted from 91 to 88 B.C., citizenship and its privileges were finally extended to the non-Roman Italians of the Republic. It was important for Virgil not to offend the Italians, who were still sensitive about the issue, so the inclusion of a list of Italian heroes was a politically wise decision.

The catalogue of Italian heroes also serves the purpose of humanizing the Italians. The individual descriptions of these men forces the reader to invest emotional energy in them, making their deaths tragic rather than deserved. This is appropriate because the war of the Italians and the Trojans is, in many ways, a civil war. Ancestrally, the Trojans are relatives of the Italians, and they will become brothers with them in the future as they marry the local women. Unfortunately, Latinus is too old to rule effectively, and Allecto is skilled at "arm[ing] brothers for battle, though they feel at one" (443-444). This further adds to the feeling of this war being a waste. Aeneas will win, but his victory will hardly be a triumph.

Study Questions

1. What simile is used to describe Amata when the snake's venom has made her mad?

2. How did Galaesus die?

3. Whom does Amata pretend has possessed her?

4. Why does Turnus enter the war?

5. Why does King Latinus offer his daughter in marriage to Aeneas?

6. Where do bees appear in this book?

7. What power does the priest Umbro have?

8. What does Latinus do when his people ask him to declare war?

9. What relatively trivial incident triggers the war?

10. Where has the image on Turnus' helmet previously appeared in the *Aeneid*?

Answers

1. She is like a top, whipped about the city.

2. He threw himself between the Trojans and Italians to try to prevent the war.

3. Amata pretends to have been possessed by Bacchus.

4. Turnus' mind is poisoned by a torch thrown at him by Allecto.

5. He has had an oracle that his daughter was to be married to a stranger.

6. The bees are omens that are interpreted to mean the arrival of foreigners.

7. Umbro can cure snake bites and cause snakes to fall asleep.

8. He shuts himself up in the palace.

9. The war is triggered by Anchises shooting Tyrrhus' pet deer.

10. The *Chimaera* was the name of one of the ships in the races of Book Five.

Suggested Essay Topics

1. The marriage of fire and fury is well developed in this book. Discuss the language Virgil uses to develop this theme as it relates to Juno, Amata, and Turnus.

2. Another unifying theme of the *Aeneid* is the movement from the old way of life to a more civilized way of life. Discuss how the Italians and their lifestyle are depicted as the older way. What is good about it, and what is bad?

Book Eight

New Characters:

Venulus: *an Italian messenger*

Tiberinus: *the god of the Tiber River*

Evander: *king of the Arcadians*

Pallas: *only son of King Evander*

Vulcan: *god of fire*

Summary

Turnus sends Venulus to Diomedes, one of the Greeks who participated in the siege of Troy, asking him to join the forces in the defense of Latium. That night, Tiberinus appears to Aeneas. He tells Aeneas not to worry, then advises him to seek an alliance with the Arcadians. He also recommends that Aeneas make sacrifices to Juno. Aeneas prays to the river in thanks, and then, spying the white sow of the prophecy, makes an offering to Juno. He then

sails upriver with two boats to find King Evander of the Arcadians. The Trojans come upon the Arcadians in the middle of a ceremony in honor of Hercules. Pallas meets them upon the river's banks and takes them to Evander. Evander willingly allies with the Trojans and invites them to join in the rites they are celebrating.

Evander tells Aeneas the story of Cacus and Hercules. Cacus, an evil monster, had been terrifying the countryside. Cacus made the mistake of stealing some of Hercules' prize cattle. Hercules ripped off the roof of Cacus' cave home, leaped inside, and strangled Cacus. In honor and thanks, the Arcadians hold an annual ceremony for Hercules.

After the ceremony, Evander explains to Aeneas the history of his land. He shows Aeneas the sites that will in the future be the sacred places and famous spaces of Rome. Evander then invites Aeneas to spend the night in his humble home.

Venus, worried about the coming war, seductively asks Vulcan to make arms for Aeneas. Vulcan agrees, and rises early the next day to direct the work on Aeneas' weapons.

Evander tells Aeneas that it would be wise for him to unite with the Etruscans, who eagerly seek to punish Mezentius for his tyranny while king of the city of Agylla. The Etruscans have been held back by the prediction that a stranger must be their leader. Unfortunately Evander is too old to lead them, and Pallas is partially Etruscan, so it falls on Aeneas to lead these men. Although Evander himself has little to offer Aeneas, he does promise to send his son and 200 horsemen with Aeneas when he leaves.

Suddenly, a vision of clashing weapons appears in the sky. Aeneas recognizes this as a warning of war sent by Venus. He sends a ship back to Ascanius, while he sets out to find the Etruscans. Evander tearfully bids good-bye to Pallas, ironically wishing to die before hearing that his son has been killed.

Venus finds Aeneas as he is camped near the Etruscans. She presents him with the beautiful armor forged for him by Vulcan. After admiring the beautiful, prophetic scenes on the shield, Aeneas hoists up his new armor, ignorant of its symbolic meaning.

Analysis

For the person unacquainted with Roman history, it is easy to sympathize with Aeneas, who finds the decorations on his shield marvelous "though he does not know what they mean" (953-955). First, the wolf with the human children is a depiction of Romulus and Remus, twin sons of Mars who were raised by a she-wolf. They have been referred to earlier in the Heroscopia as well as Jupiter's prediction to Venus in Book One. There follows a reference to the Rape of the Sabine Women, when the Romans carried the daughters of the neighboring Sabines off to be their wives. The shield is also covered with famous episodes from the time of the kings and scenes of the Republican wars showing a Rome that punishes lawless violence and reveres (and is protected by) the gods.

The center of the shield is dominated by a glorified depiction of Augustus' defeat of Antony and Cleopatra at Actium. As at Troy, the gods fight overhead. The shield attempts to convey the end to the years of civil war that had torn Rome and the subsequent rise of a golden age. Many versions of the *Aeneid* have glossaries that describe in detail the shield.

This famous set piece is a blatant imitation of the *Iliad*'s lengthy description of the shield of Achilles. Achilles' shield depicted scenes of marriage, festivals, and death as well as scenes of war. The implication was that these were all things that Achilles would miss because of his early death. Hence, the shield lent a tragic tone to the *Iliad*. In contrast, the shield of Aeneas overwhelmingly shows scenes of victory. He is one of a line of heroes stretching from Hercules to Augustus who "resorts to force only to curtail the destructive, utterly negative results of Disorder" (Anderson, 73). The effect is triumphant, and nicely allows Virgil to praise the peace Augustus had established.

In the description of the bucolic lifestyle of the Arcadians, Virgil has created a scene that appealed to the Roman nostalgia for simpler times and ways of life. The Arcadians also illustrate the theme of the replacement of old ways by new as much as do the primitive Italian heroes. The Arcadians are morally superior to many of the Italian forces. They are pious, as can be seen from their many places of worship, and they have no love for wealth.

(Avarice will become the sin which brings down many warriors in the following books.) Finally, Evander's walking tour of his kingdom provides a link between the Rome of old and the Rome of the present. Much as Virgil gave added weight to the religious institutions of Rome by showing them being founded by the mighty Aeneas, his description of the Roman religious sites being utilized in ancient times could have only added to a Roman's feeling of awe.

Study Questions

1. How does Virgil describe Tiberinus?

2. What offering does Aeneas make to Juno?

3. Why does Evander recognize Aeneas?

4. How does Cacus attempt to hide the location of the cattle he steals?

5. How do Hercules' troubles parallel Aeneas'?

6. How did Cacus decorate the outside of his cave?

7. Why is Mezentius no longer on his throne?

8. Who forges Aeneas' wonderful armor?

9. What two people does Augustus face at Actium?

10. What different names are given for the forces whose aid Aeneas seeks?

Answers

1. Tiberinus is dressed in sea-green linen, with a crown of reeds on his head.

2. He offers her the white sow and her 30 piglets.

3. Evander had met Anchises long ago and saw the family resemblance in Aeneas.

4. He makes the cattle walk backward into his cave.

5. Both Aeneas and Hercules are plagued by the angry Juno.

6. Cacus' cave had men's heads hung outside of it.

7. Mezentius was ejected from his kingdom for his tyranny.

8. Aeneas' armor is forged by Vulcan, who is technically his stepfather.

9. Augustus is fighting against Antony and Cleopatra.

10. They are called Tuscans, Etruscans, Etrurians, Maeonia's sons, and Lydians.

Suggested Essay Topics

1. The story of Hercules is a metaphor for Aeneas' trials in Italy. What parallels exist between his tale and Hercules? Without knowing the end of the tale, what does Aeneas' arrival promise for the Italians?

2. Compare the shield of Aeneas to the Heroscopia. How do the two predictions differ? What does each imply about Aeneas' role in his new community as well as in Rome?

Book Nine

New Characters:

Cybele: *the mother goddess*

Numanus: *brother-in-law of Turnus, taunter of the Trojans*

Apollo: *god of the sun*

Pandarus and Bitias: *twin Trojan giants*

Summary

Juno sends Iris to Turnus. Iris tells Turnus that Aeneas is not in the Trojan camp and urges him to take the opportunity to attack. Turnus offers prayers of thanks, happily obeying the goddess who sent him this news.

The Italian forces advance on the Trojans, who retreat to their fortress as Aeneas ordered. Turnus throws the first javelin, symbolically starting the attack. Unable to penetrate the walls, he turns his energy to the Trojan's ships. These ships were built of wood from a grove sacred to Cybele. Jupiter had promised her that he would protect the trees if they were attacked after they made it to Italy. As Turnus attempts to burn the fleet, the ships dive beneath the waves and reappear as sea nymphs.

Turnus rallies his disturbed troops, ignoring the meaning of the ships' transformation. He reminds them that the Trojans have stolen his promised bride just as Paris stole Helen, implying that Troy will fall yet again. His forces blockade the gates for the night.

On watch as sentries, Nisus and Euryalus agree to try to cross the Italian lines to reach Aeneas. Ascanius promises them great presents if they return, but Euryalus only wants assurances that his mother will be cared for should he die.

Moving through the camp, Nisus and Euryalus mercilessly slaughter the sleeping Italians. Euryalus takes the golden armor of Rhamnes, and he and Nisus leave for safer ground. As they depart, a troop of horsemen led by Volcens sees light reflecting off Euryalus' helmet. The two Trojans attempt to escape in the forest, but Euryalus gets lost and is caught. Nisus spears two of his friend's captors, for which Euryalus is killed by the angry Volcens. Nisus then rushes the Italians, managing to kill Volcens before he, too, is killed. Virgil concludes their story with a promise to preserve their memory forever.

The next day, the Latin captains parade in front of the Trojans walls, displaying the heads of Nisus and Euryalus on pikes. Euryalus' mother hears of her son's death and rushes to the walls, broken-hearted. She is carried away in the arms of two of the Trojan defenders.

The Italian forces attack the Trojan's walls, which the Trojans defend in a well-practiced way. Turnus sets a tower aflame, which collapses, killing all within but two. Death is dealt on all sides. Ascanius makes his first kill, shooting Numanus Remulus, who had been calling the Trojans Phrygian women. Apollo then appears and tells Ascanius to remove himself from the fighting.

Pandarus and Bitias open the gates, tempting the Italians to enter. Trojans attack and hold off the intruders, then makes sallies outside. Turnus hears of the open gate and races for it, slaughtering as he goes.

Mars then encourages the Latins and instills fear to the Trojans. Pandarus heaves the gate shut, accidentally locking Turnus inside. Turnus kills Pandarus, then attacks as many Trojans as he can find. A panic ensues in the fort, but fortunately Turnus' bloodlust keeps him from thinking of opening the gates. The Trojans finally unite, pushing Turnus back. Jupiter tells Juno to stop helping Turnus, and Turnus finally leaps into the Tiber and escapes.

Analysis

Most of the drama of the last four books of the *Aeneid* is based upon the conflict between Aeneas and Turnus. Rather than portraying Turnus as a one-dimensional nemesis, Virgil has chosen to make him a sympathetic character. Turnus might not have chosen to fight without the intervention of Allecto, but his declared reason is noble: he is fighting to protect his homeland from foreign invaders and regain his chosen bride. He is handsome and an excellent warrior. The similes Virgil uses to describe him are uniformly complementary.

Turnus is a tragic character. The prophecies throughout the book have made it evident that it is not possible for him to win the war. His own characterization of the Italian situation as parallel to that of the Greeks in their war against the Trojans is false: Lavinia is not a stolen wife, it was Hector who burnt the Greek boats, and it is now Aeneas who has the sacred armor. Turnus does not realize that his role in this drama is to be Hector, not Achilles. Fate is now allied with the Trojans. Turnus' goddess-induced madness for war and his noble character ultimately will undermine the glory of the Trojan victory.

Turnus also lacks one of the vital personal characteristics of the ideal Roman leader: he does not have self-restraint. This problem, emphasized through Virgil's use of animal similes, is most apparent in Turnus' failure to open the gates of the Trojan fortress. While his blood-lust appeals to Mars, it keeps Turnus from taking the action which could have actually defeated his enemies. Turnus is definitely a good warrior, but his style of leadership is not the kind that could lead the Italian people to greatness. For that, they will need the self-discipline epitomized by Aeneas. Turnus is a great man who is about to become obsolete.

Nisus and Euryalus' decision to kill the sleeping Italians instead of heading directly to Aeneas shows the same kind of disastrous rashness. However, their devoted friendship is the epitome of the highest of Roman social virtues. In the footrace of Book Five, their friendship benefits them both; in this book, it is their undoing.

It is interesting to note the elaborate introduction Virgil provides these two characters, as if they had not previously been in the book. This discrepancy is one of the reasons that Book Five is believed to have been inserted after most of the *Aeneid* had been written. (The other discrepancy is the difference between Book Five's account of the death of Palinarus, and another version in Book Six.) It is believed that Virgil would have corrected this problem if he had lived to edit his own work. As it stands, the "errors" have provided plenty of fodder for scholarly discussion.

Study Questions

1. What is Turnus compared to as he paces the Trojan's walls?

2. What does Euryalus say is a cheap price for honor?

3. Why does Euryalus not bid his mother good-bye?

4. What three things foreshadow the death of Nisus and Euryalus?

5. What final attempt does Nisus make to save his friend?

6. What two gods are used in the simile describing Turnus hauling a Trojan down from the fort's walls?

7. Why doesn't Bitias' spear hit Turnus?

8. What simile is used to describe the death of the giant Bitias?

9. What mistake does Turnus make once within the Trojan camp?

10. How does the Tiber respond to Turnus' dive?

Answers

1. He is compared to a starving wolf at a sheep pen.

2. He says life is a cheap price for honor.

3. He says he could not stand against her tears.

4. First, Nisus says he would prefer that Euryalus survive him if there were some disaster. Second, Euryalus provides for his mother in case of his death. Finally, the narrative says, as they depart, that the tidings Ascanius gives the pair for Aeneas are "useless offerings" (416).

5. Nisus shows himself to the Italian horsemen after Volcens says he will punish Euryalus in place of the person who had just killed two members of his troop.

6. Turnus is likened to Jove's eagle or Mars' wolf.

7. Juno's intervention protects Turnus from Bitias' spear.

8. He is likened to a stone pier falling into the ocean.

9. Turnus does not open the gates to let his companion in.

10. The river welcomes Turnus.

Suggested Essay Topics

1. Examine the two episodes involving Nisus and Euryalus. Are the apparent discrepancies mistakes or deliberate literary choices? If mistakes, what do you think was Virgil's intended version and intended message? If deliberate, what underlying message was Virgil trying to convey?

2. Compare Turnus to Aeneas. How are their characters different? How has Virgil made each of them sympathetic? Examine their words and actions as well as the similes Virgil uses to describe them.

Book Ten

New Characters:

Cymodoce: *chief of the nymphs formed from Aeneas' ships*

Tarchon: *leader of the Etruscan Agyllans*

Lausus: *son of Mezentius*

Magus: *an Italian fighting for Turnus*

Orodes: *a Trojan soldier*

Summary

Jupiter has called a conference in Olympus. He says that it is time for there to be peace in Italy. Venus reminds Jupiter that the Trojans have only been following the oracles of the gods. She implicitly blames Juno for the current state of war. Juno denies that she has anything to do with the current Trojan troubles. She adds that, considering what Venus can do for the Trojans, it is only fair for others to aid the Italians.

The gods are divided over which goddess to support. Jupiter steps in, declaring that from now on the Trojans and Italians will have to fight without supernatural help.

While the Trojans continue the defense of their walls, Aeneas is sailing to meet them, followed by the newly allied Tuscans. Virgil describes these people and their ships in the Catalogue of the Etruscan Allies. Cymodoce climbs the stern of Aeneas' boat and warns him of the trouble facing his people, pushing his boat ahead as she leaves.

Seeing the approach of the fleet the next morning, the Trojan forces rally within their enclosure. Turnus attempts to cut off the Etruscans while they are landing, but Tarchon decides to sacrifice the boats' hulls in order to land more quickly. Aeneas cuts a bloody swath through the Italians. Venus turns aside a few weapons that might otherwise have hit him.

Pallas gives his forces an encouraging speech, then plunges into the thickest mass of the Latin forces. While he valiantly kills Latins, his own Arcadians begin to take serious casualties. Turnus comes to the Latins' aid, meeting Pallas in personal combat. Pallas prays to Hercules for help, but Hercules can do nothing. Turnus kills Pallas, then strips off his beautiful sword belt.

Aeneas hears that the Trojans desperately need assistance and that Pallas has died. Enraged, he goes in search of Turnus, leaving death in his wake. He refuses pleas for mercy and even curses a man he has killed.

In light of Venus' interference, Jupiter allows Juno to save

Turnus, with the understanding that Turnus will not be able to escape his impending death. Juno then creates a phantom Aeneas, which Turnus chases across the battlefield. The figure runs up the gangplank of a boat. As soon as Turnus is aboard, Juno makes the boat sail away, to Turnus' distress. Juno keeps him from either swimming back to land or killing himself in shame.

Mezentius takes up the fight for the Latins. The slaughter becomes widespread; neither side has the advantage.

Aeneas and Mezentius meet. Aeneas' lance strikes a non-fatal blow. He comes after Mezentius with his sword, but Lausus leaps in to save his father. Lausus' companions join him against Aeneas, and Mezentius manages to retreat. Aeneas is angered and kills Lausus. As Lausus dies, Aeneas suddenly feels pity for the boy's devotion to his father. He allows Lausus' body to be carried away.

Mezentius is agonized that his son died in his place. He rides back to face Aeneas. Aeneas kills Mezentius' horse, which traps Mezentius beneath its body as it falls. Before Aeneas strikes, Mezentius asks one favor only: to be buried next to his son. He then allows himself to be killed.

Analysis

Filled with battle scenes, Book Ten seems an endless catalogue of slaughter. Virgil attempts to break the role call of gory deaths by inserting conversations between the gods and the list of the Etruscan heroes. While Virgil seeks to create variety by giving every victim a novel, although invariably bloody death, the list of names and alliances finally becomes a blur. With the gods out of the way, the Trojans and Italians are essentially equal, dying equally painfully and in equally great numbers.

Such ambivalence extends to the characterizations of Book Ten. Aeneas commits unholy actions, the godless Mezentius behaves with honor, and Turnus is ready to kill himself because he has been removed from the battle. None of these three characters is all hero or all villain, and the reader is confused by the difficulty in supporting any of them whole-heartedly. Aeneas may have destiny on his side, but Turnus gains sympathy because he is fighting against destiny and for a just cause. Mezentius, the man who tied the living to the dead, on the battlefield becomes a man who fights fairly and loves his son deeply. Virgil, by not dehumanizing Aeneas' antagonists, has made his work richer.

In contrast to these three men, Lausus and Pallas have much less depth. Both of them are young, handsome, and doomed to die on the battlefield. Both of them dedicate their deaths to their fathers, one in speech and the other in action. They are part of a recurring motif of untimely deaths that Virgil uses effectively to convey the message that war, while often necessary, is still a great tragedy. Virgil's underlying desire for peace is completely in tune with the sentiments of his original audience.

Study Questions

1. Whose prophecies does Juno say the Aeneidae have been following?

2. Why is Pallas not afraid of Turnus?

3. How does Pallas' belt mirror Pallas' own fate?

4. Why does Hercules cry?

5. What curse does Aeneas pronounce over Tarquitus' corpse?

6. Who is Turnus' sister?

7. Why is Juno allowed to interfere in the battle?

8. Give two similes used to describe Mezentius on the battle-field.

9. Why is Aeneas distressed by the death of Lausus?

10. What is Mezentius' last wish?

Answers

1. She says they have been following "the prophecies of mad Cassandra" (93).

2. Whether he dies or conquers Turnus, he will have won glory. For this reason, Turnus' threats do not scare him.

3. Like the bridegrooms, Pallas will be cut off in his youth.

4. He wants to help Pallas, but Jupiter will not let him.

5. He curses him to never be buried, but to be eaten by birds or fishes.

6. Turnus' sister is the nymph Juturna.

7. Juno is allowed to save Turnus because Venus has protected Aeneas.

8. Mezentius is compared to a hunted boar and a starved lion.

9. Aeneas is impressed by the boy's devotion to his father.

10. Mezentius' last wish is to be buried beside his son.

Suggested Essay Topics

1. While Turnus is the "bad guy" in the *Aeneid*, Aeneas becomes a force of disorder in this book—or does he? Examine the actions and words of Aeneas as well as his narrative description to determine whether or not Aeneas has become the antagonist in Book Ten.

2. Examine the characters of Pallas and Lausus. How are they similar? How are they different? What symbolic role do they fill in the book?

Book Eleven

New Characters:

Drances: *an elderly Latin who is opposed to Turnus*

Diana: *goddess of the hunt, Camilla's patron*

Opis: *a member of Diana's troop of maiden huntresses*

Arruns: *an Etruscan fighter*

Summary

Before returning Pallas' body to Evander, Aeneas builds a trophy for Mars, decorated with the arms of Mezentius. Aeneas mourns over Pallas, then arranges to have an honor guard accompany his body. Even Pallas' horse is crying.

The Latins ask Aeneas for permission to collect their dead.

Aeneas willingly grants it, adding that these deaths would not have occurred if Turnus had challenged him to personal combat and let the gods pick the winner. Drances agrees to bring Aeneas' offer back to King Latinus. A truce is declared.

Pallas' body arrives in Arcadia. Evander is overwrought. He consoles himself, reminding himself that his son died in battle and killed many before he died. He tells the Trojans attending Pallas to return to Aeneas with the message that Aeneas owes him and Pallas Turnus' life.

The funerals of the Latins run for days. The greatest mourning occurs in Laurentum, where many feel that this war is a personal matter of Turnus' and should be settled between him and Aeneas.

Venulus returns from the kingdom of Diomedes. Not only has Diomedes declined to enter into an alliance against the Trojans, he has advised the Latins to join with Aeneas. This news upsets the gathered Latin council.

Latinus proposes to the assembly that the Trojans be offered peace and some land to settle on, or a new fleet if they desire to leave. Drances says that it is clear that this war has come about because of Turnus' pride, and that Turnus should either accept defeat or challenge Aeneas directly. Turnus says that he has not been defeated, and that the Latins should continue fighting. However, he adds, if it is a duel that is needed, he will do it for the good of the Latin people.

Suddenly a messenger arrives, announcing that the combined Trojan and Tuscan forces are descending on the city. Turnus quickly organizes the defense of the city. He is met outside of the city by Camilla, who offers to attack the invaders first. Turnus assigns her to lead the Italian squadrons while he prepares a trap for Aeneas in a forested valley.

Diana is unhappy about her inability to protect Camilla. Long ago, Camilla's father, who had been exiled from his kingdom, was being hunted down by his enemies. As he prepared to swim a flooding river, he suddenly feared for the safety of his infant daughter. With a prayer to dedicate her to Diana, he affixed Camilla to a lance and flung it safely across the waters. Raised in the woods, Camilla grew to be a great huntress, dearly beloved by her patroness. Diana therefore sends Opis to avenge Camilla's death and retrieve her body for burial.

The Trojan forces meet the Latins in a mighty clash of javelins and cavalry. The battle goes back and forth, with both sides suffering heavy losses. Camilla kills one man after another. Jupiter inspires Tarchon to fight. He then drags Venulus off of his horse, greatly encouraging the Tuscans.

In the midst of the chaos, Arruns hunts down Camilla. Camilla, in her single-minded tracking of a brightly armored former priest, forgets to pay attention to her surroundings. With the aid of a prayer to Apollo, Arruns' lance strikes Camilla down. As her dying wish, Camilla requests that Turnus be told to drive the Trojans from Laurentum.

Opis locates Arruns, who is full of pride at his deed. She shoots him with her bow. His comrades abandon him and run.

The Latins, exhausted, begin to retreat. The city gates are closed, shutting some Trojans in and some Latins out. Hearing of the panic, Turnus leaves his ambush in the forest. Aeneas enters the pass almost immediately upon Turnus' departure. They catch sight of each other as night falls.

Analysis

This book continues the battles that lead to the inevitable encounter of Turnus and Aeneas. Virgil's battle scenes are considered inferior to his lyrical moments, such as his descriptions of the shield of Aeneas. Nonetheless, Book Eleven is enlightened by the presence of Camilla, who, with her "shepherd's pike of myrtle tipped with steel" is the epitome of the native fighting spirit of the Italians (VII: 1072).

Camilla's story is remarkable, but her death is inevitable. First, as a shepherd-huntress, she is another member of the individualistic society which is about to be supplanted. Second, as a beautiful, valorous youth, she is destined for the same tragic fate as Pallas and Lausus. Finally, Camilla's flaw, her "female's love of plunder and spoils," condemns her just as it has Euryalus and just as it will Turnus (1038-1039). Aeneas dedicates all of his plunder to the gods.

But Camilla's spirit lives on as an inspiration to the women of

Laurentum, who defend their city with "sturdy oak clubs and charred stakes," as well as in the valor of Cloelia, the Roman hostage who swam the Tiber to escape captivity (as depicted on Aeneas' shield). There may be no room for Amazonian maidens in the new society, but it will be these brave, patriotic women who form its bloodstock.

In the speeches of Turnus and Drances, it is interesting to note that Turnus, who criticizes Drances for being long-winded, rambles for nearly twice as long as Drances. Furthermore, rather than listening to Drances' wise advice, Turnus seizes upon the disorder caused by the impending arrival of the Trojan forces to lead yet another war party against them, a move which causes further, unnecessary bloodshed. His actions contrast strongly with that of Aeneas, who, as shown in his speech to the Latin ambassadors, has respect for the human cost of war and wants to limit its destructiveness. Turnus' flawed leadership skills, which are marked by rashness and a focus on personal pride over the good of the group, have their final glorious failure in his abandonment of the ambush. Turnus is a noble warrior, but he is clearly not the man who will lead the Latin people to glory.

Virgil emphasizes these aspects of Turnus in the simile of the freed stallion. Borrowed from the *Iliad*, the simile was used by Homer to describe Paris and Hector in their irresponsible moments. As Anderson explains, Turnus is unhesitating, action-oriented, and handsome, which are all positive attributes. Yet, much as the stallion's place is in the stable, Turnus' place is at the council table. Rather than choosing to indulge himself in more fighting, Turnus should have responsibly accepted a duel with Aeneas.

Study Questions

1. What does Diomedes say has been the fate of the Greeks who participated in the Trojan War?

2. Along with gold and ivory, what gift does Latinus want presented to the Trojans?

3. Why does Evander want Aeneas to avenge Pallas' death?

4. What difference is there between the Trojan and the Latin funerals?

5. How does Turnus insult Drances?

6. What metaphor is used to describe Turnus?

7. What aid do the gods improperly offer during the meeting of the forces outside of Laurentum?

8. What metaphor is used to describe the struggle between Tarchon and Venulus?

9. What second big opportunity does Turnus' rage cause him to bungle?

10. How does Virgil poetically indicate the end of the day?

Answers

1. He says that they have all had bad luck. As examples he cites Agamemnon, who was killed by his wife, and his own companions, who were transformed into birds.

2. He wants his throne and robe—"the emblems of my sovereignty"—presented to the Trojans (442).

3. First, Evander cannot do it himself. Second, he wishes to tell Pallas' shade, when he joins him in the underworld, that Turnus is dead.

4. While the Trojans are cremated with honors, including sacrifices and honor guards, most of the Latins are simply heaped up in piles and set aflame.

5. Turnus says that Drances has always preferred speaking even when fighting was necessary, and then reminds the assembly that Drances has killed no Trojans. Implicitly, Turnus is calling Drances a blustering coward.

6. He is like a stallion that has snapped its tether.

7. Jupiter encourages Tarchon and forces Turnus out of the forest, while Apollo enables Arruns to strike Camilla.

8. They are like a snake and an eagle fighting in the air.

9. By leaving the forest, he misses his chance to kill Aeneas.

10. He says that Phoebus (Apollo) is bathing his weary horses in the Spanish (western) sea.

Suggested Essay Topics

1. Examine the varied references to the gods in this book. How does the inclusion of these supernatural forces affect the book? What messages is Virgil conveying through their use?

2. Analyze the portrait of King Latinus painted by Virgil. How is he made to appear a man whose time to rule has passed?

Book Twelve

New Characters:

Juturna: *Turnus' sister, goddess of pools and rivers*

Tolumnius: *the Rutulians' auger*

Iapyx: *Aeneas' healer*

Summary

Turnus is eager to fight Aeneas, and asks Latinus to prepare a peace treaty before the duel. Latinus asks Turnus to consider not fighting. He tells him there are plenty of marriageable girls available, that he knew it was wrong to offer Lavinia to any of her suitors because of the oracles, and that, if peace can be had, he is sure that he can have peace and also have Turnus alive.

Turnus says that glory is too important to him for him to not fight. Queen Amata then begs him not to fight, as she is sure that her fortunes will fall with him. Seeing Lavinia blush, Turnus goes wild with love for her. He sends a messenger to tell Aeneas to meet him at dawn.

The next morning, the troops gather on the field to watch the confrontation. In Olympus, Juno warns Juturna that her brother is about to die, encouraging her to try to save him, or at least incite a war that will break the treaty. Back in Latium, Latinus and Aeneas meet in front of the sacrificial altar, where Aeneas prays, promising that he will treat the Italians as equals if he wins, preserving their religious traditions and customs. Latinus also prays, promising to uphold the treaty under any circumstances.

The Rutulians are unhappy about the apparently unequal

nature of this duel. While they watch the nervous, pale Turnus pace back and forth, Juturna enters their ranks disguised as one of their most distinguished fighters. She encourages them to attack. To further incite them, she makes an omen appear in the sky. Tolumnius interprets it as a sign to defend Turnus and throws a lance at the Trojans and their allies. Soon, war breaks out again. Aeneas tries to restrain his warriors, but he is hit by an arrow thrown by an unknown hand and is carried off the field. Seeing Aeneas fall back, Turnus leaps into his chariot and attacks.

In Aeneas' camp, Iapyx attempts vainly to remove the arrowhead. Venus secretly mixes a plant into Iapyx's salves which causes the arrowhead to leap out and the wound to instantaneously heal. Aeneas then rearms and leaves to find Turnus.

Juturna disguises herself as her brother's charioteer, taking his place behind the horses. While she skillfully keeps her brother from Aeneas, Aeneas grows tired of Turnus' treachery. He finally decides to enter the battle. Aeneas and Turnus wreak violent death across the plains until Venus inspires Aeneas to directly attack the city. As the city starts to burn, Amata hangs herself.

Turnus grows tired of racing in his chariot. Juturna tries to convince him not to return to the city, but he recognizes her. A messenger rides up and begs Turnus to come to Laurentum, lest it be entirely destroyed. Turnus walks away from the chariot and goes to the city walls. As he calls for a halt to the fighting, both sides stop and clear a space for the two warriors to meet.

The duel starts as both men hurl spears. They then rush at each other with their swords. Unevenly matched against Vulcan's smithery, Turnus' blade snaps off. Turnus runs to get a replacement while Aeneas chases him. Aeneas attempts to remove his spear from a tree trunk in order to throw it at his now-moving target, but Faunus hears Turnus' prayers and holds the metal tightly. Juturna tosses her brother his sword. This angers Venus, who frees Aeneas' spear from the tree.

Jupiter, seeing Juno watching the battle below, chastises her for her interference. He tells her that she is no longer allowed to harass the Trojans. She says that she had indeed given up her war. She only asks that after the Trojans unite with the Latins, that the Latins not adopt the Trojan ways and that the name of Troy die forever. Jupiter agrees, adding that the two races mingled will be known as Latins.

Jupiter then sends down a Fury to drive Juturna away from the combat. Disguised as a bird, the Fury terrifies Turnus by flying in his face. Juturna recognizes the creature and dives, despairing, into a river.

Turnus attempts to hit Aeneas with a giant rock, but his strength seems to have left him and the rock misses. While Turnus wavers, Aeneas throws a spear that hits Turnus in the thigh. Turnus concedes the victory to Aeneas, and requests that he be returned to his father, if not alive, then dead.

Aeneas contemplates sparing Turnus' life. As he is about to grant clemency, he spots Pallas' sword belt gleaming off of Turnus' shoulders. In Pallas' name, the enraged Aeneas buries his sword in Turnus' chest. Turnus' soul escapes and flees to the underworld.

Analysis

After the endless battles of the preceding books, the ending of the *Aeneid* seems anticlimactic. Where is the triumphant wedding scene? When does Virgil allow Aeneas to enjoy what he has struggled to achieve? If nothing else, why focus on Turnus' stiffening body and resentful soul? It is hardly a glorious ending.

The debate over Virgil's choice rages on over 2,000 years after it was written. William S. Anderson says that Aeneas' killing of Turnus is simply a human tragedy. Aeneas cannot win a victory whether he saves Turnus, who deserves it as a suppliant and man of honor, or kills him. The point of this ambiguous moral situation is that it parallels the foundation of Rome. Rome was morally compromised; the welcomed Augustan peace was accompanied by doubtful means of restoring order. Virgil's ambiguity is "a vehicle for conveying his complex vision of Rome" (Anderson, 108).

Michael Putnam contrasts his interpretation to that of the historicists, whose opinions have dominated the literature. To them, the *Aeneid* is "a grandly imaginative reinforcement of Augustan ideology and power structures" (Putnam, 2). Aeneas kills Turnus because it is good and right for the Roman forces to triumph. But for Putnam, Virgil encoded more than one meaning into his ending. Although he has been told by Anchises that the city his children will found will spare the defeated, Aeneas chooses instead to let his desire for revenge run unchecked as the sight of Pallas' belt draws him down from his statesman-like hesitation to the dirty world of practical politics. Turnus' death therefore foretells not peace, but war and an end to liberty, while Aeneas' failure shows that he has not brought the perfection of Olympus down to the mortal plane.

Virgil does demonstrate his masterful abilities of organization in the last book. Two elements of the final scene match up with those of the first, in essence providing bookends. In the first book, it is Aeneas whose "limbs fall slack with chill" and stretches his hands in prayer; in the last scene of the *Aeneid*, Turnus follows both of these actions. Also, in the opening of the book, Juno is burning with rage and the desire for revenge; in the final book, Aeneas is the one filled with such a rage. To Putnam, this transformation of the protagonist into a god-like figure who imitates the actions of his former nemesis is full of tension, especially because of the similarity between Turnus' death and that of Hector's.

Turnus' death confuses the interpretation of the *Aeneid's* meaning in many ways. Turnus is constantly incapacitated by fury, which is associated with Juno and other violent characters. Thus, Aeneas' victory can be seen as the triumph of order over chaos and the irrational. Yet in the end, it is Aeneas who is possessed by fury as he sees Pallas' belt. It is as if his ability to exercise rational rule will no longer be exercised now that he is the dominant one. Aeneas has also been interpreted as the man who brings civilization to the Italians. Yet, the nobility of the Italians and Aeneas' failure to live up to Anchises' prediction bring into doubt whether Rome's glories have really resulted in a better way of life. The Italians certainly fought better, but would it not have been preferable to have maintained the honest, pastoral life of the Arcadians?

The *Aeneid* is also seen as a tale of rewarded suffering. Aeneas pays terribly for his obedience to the will of the gods, and he is ultimately given a kingdom and a home for his people. However, Turnus also is fighting for a just cause, and his reward is death. Is the overall tone therefore one of optimism or pessimism? Rather than providing easy answers, Virgil forces the reader to consider the options and decide for himself or herself. As Putnam says, "It is this realistic appraisal of Rome and of life's ultimate ambivalence—the glory but also finally the tragedy—that at the present time continues to earn for the *Aeneid* its status as a masterpiece" (Putnam, 26).

Study Questions

1. Who tries to discourage Turnus from fighting?

2. What sign does Juturna make appear in the sky?

3. How do Aeneas' and Turnus' responses to the disintegration of the truce differ?

4. What simile is used to describe Turnus as he races around in his chariot?

5. What simile describes Aeneas as he leads his troops back on the field?

6. What sign tells Turnus that his plans in Laurentum are all to come to nothing?

7. What other character dies exactly as Turnus dies ("with a moan...fled to shades below")?

8. What animal simile is used for both Turnus and Aeneas?

9. Why does Juturna curse her status as an immortal?

10. Who does Lavinia say she wants to win?

Answers

1. Both Latinus and Amata try to make Turnus change his mind.

2. She makes an eagle, who has just caught a swan, drop the swan after a flock of birds attacks it.

3. Aeneas tries to restrain his men, while Turnus sees the fighting as an opportunity for more fighting.

4. He is like Mars racing along the Hebrus, accompanied by Fear, Anger, and Stratagem.

5. He is like an approaching storm that makes the farmers fear

for their crops.

6. Watching the city burning from the field, Turnus sees a tower he had built engulfed in flames.

7. Camilla's death scene uses exactly the same language.

8. They are likened to two bulls fighting for control of a herd. The bull simile is also used earlier in the book to describe Turnus.

9. Juturna is unhappy at facing life without her brother and wishes she could accompany him into the underworld.

10. Lavinia says nothing and expresses no opinions throughout the book.

Suggested Essay Topics

1. This book has the second most references to the *Iliad*. If you have read the *Iliad*, explain these similarities in detail. Does Virgil succeed in his desire to become the Roman Homer, or does he fall short?

2. Could Turnus have been allowed to survive? Discuss why or why not.

Sample Analytical Paper Topics

Topic #1

    Trace the course of fury and its accompanying fire-based language as used in the *Aeneid*. Discuss fury in the characters of Juno, Dido, and Turnus. What is its role in the book? Include an analysis of the fury of Aeneas in the final book.

Outline

I.   Thesis Statement: *In the* Aeneid, *fury is a recurring theme, often occurring with descriptions of fire. The fury of Juno, Dido, and Turnus makes them weak and irrational and increases sympathy for Aeneas and his eventual success. However, Aeneas' domination by fury at the end of the* Aeneid *mars his moment of triumph.*

II.   Fury and Juno

    A.   Examples of Juno's fury

    B.   Juno's irrational actions

    C.   Juno's anger causes her to attempt to subvert fate, leading to the destruction of her mortal favorites.

III.   Fury and Dido

    A.   Dido's "burning" love

    B.   Dido's fury at Aeneas' planned departure

    C. Dido's irrational actions

    D. Dido's fury and burning love cause her to act irresponsibly, causing the collapse of her ability to rule and leading to her own destruction.

IV. Fury and Turnus

    A. Allecto's flame

    B. Turnus' fury in war

    C. Turnus' irresponsible actions

    D. While Turnus' fury helps to make him a good warrior, it causes him to make mistakes that bring about his downfall.

V. Fury and Aeneas

    A. Juno

        1. Juno's fury is irrational and destructive.

        2. Juno increases sympathy for Aeneas, who continues to piously make offerings to her.

    B. Dido

        1. Aeneas' ability to leave "burning" Dido increases sympathy for Aeneas as a pious man

        2. Dido's fury inspired irresponsibility contrasts strongly with Aeneas' consistent care for his people.

    C. Turnus

        1. Turnus' irresponsible actions contrast strongly with Aeneas' calm decisions.

        2. The reader concludes that Aeneas would be the better leader of Italy.

VI. Conclusion: Aeneas' fury

    A. After Aeneas has been shown consistently to be responsible and rational, his actions at the end of the book are only the pious fulfillment of a promise made to Pallas' father.

B.   While his fury is unfortunate, his actions are those a king must take to preserve the peace.

Topic #2

Predictive dreams occur frequently in the *Aeneid*. Examine Aeneas' dream of Hector and Turnus' dream of Allecto. How are they similar? What comparisons do they invite the reader to draw?

Outline

I.   Thesis Statement: *The similar dreams of Aeneas and Turnus simultaneously introduce the different characters of the two men and tell the reader of their fates.*

II.   Aeneas' dream

    A.   Description of dream

    B.   The parting gesture of Hector

    C.   Aeneas' predicted future

III.   Turnus' dream

    A.   Description of dream

    B.   The parting gesture of Allecto

    C.   Turnus' predicted future

IV.   Comparison of dreams and dreamers

    A.   Comparison of dreams

        1.   Only dreams with dialogue between dreamers and dream

        2.   Neither dreamer wants to believe the predictions

        3.   Both end with the dreamer given something by a messenger

        4.   Both end with simile illuminating character of dreamer

    B.   Comparison of dreamers

        1.   Dreamers treat messengers differently

2.   Different similes show different characters

a.   Aeneas' concern is for his people

b.   Turnus acts impulsively to fight

Topic #3

Is the evolution of Aeneas' character positive or negative? Be sure to include actions that could indicate a conclusion opposite to your own and resolve the conflict they create in your proposed interpretation.

Outline

I.   Thesis Statement: *Aeneas evolves positively/negatively over the course of the* Aeneid.

II.   Aeneas' positive evolution

A.   Accepts his destiny

B.   Leaves behind his tainted past

C.   Becomes a better leader

III.   Impediments to positive view

A.   Behavior on battlefield

B.   Desertion of Dido

C.   Murder of suppliant Turnus

IV.   Resolution of inconsistent behavior

A.   Aeneas must kill; it is weak to ask for mercy.

B.   Aeneas is piously obeying the will of the gods when he leaves Carthage.

C.   Aeneas' anger shows he is only human; Turnus would have been a threat if he had lived.

SECTION FOUR

Bibliography

Anderson, William S. *The Art of the Aeneid.* 1969. New Jersey: Prentice Hall.

Davenport, Basil. *The Portable Roman Reader.* 1951. New York: Viking Press.

Kragelund, Patrick. *Dream and Prediction in the Aeneid.* 1976. Denmark: Special Trykkeriet.

Pope, Nancy P. *National History in the Heroic Poem: A Comparison of the Aeneid and The Faerie Queene.* 1990. New York: Garland Publishing.

Putnam, Michael C. J. *Virgil's Aeneid: Interpretation and Influence.* 1995. Chapel Hill: University of North Carolina Press.

Slavit, David R. *Virgil.* 1991. New Haven: Yale University Press.

—*Aeneid.* Translated by Allen Mandelbaum (1964) 197. New York: Bantam Books.

—*Aeneidos Liber Quintus.* Edited with commentary by R. D. Williams. 1960. Oxford: Clarendon Press.

Williams, R. D. *The Aeneid of Virgil.* 1985. Bristol: Bristol Classics.

REA's **Problem Solvers**

The "PROBLEM SOLVERS" are comprehensive supplemental textbooks designed to save time in finding solutions to problems. Each "PROBLEM SOLVER" is the first of its kind ever produced in its field. It is the product of a massive effort to illustrate almost any imaginable problem in exceptional depth, detail, and clarity. Each problem is worked out in detail with a step-by-step solution, and the problems are arranged in order of complexity from elementary to advanced. Each book is fully indexed for locating problems rapidly.

ACCOUNTING	LINEAR ALGEBRA
ADVANCED CALCULUS	MACHINE DESIGN
ALGEBRA & TRIGONOMETRY	MATHEMATICS for ENGINEERS
AUTOMATIC CONTROL	MECHANICS
SYSTEMS/ROBOTICS	NUMERICAL ANALYSIS
BIOLOGY	OPERATIONS RESEARCH
BUSINESS, ACCOUNTING, & FINANCE	OPTICS
CALCULUS	ORGANIC CHEMISTRY
CHEMISTRY	PHYSICAL CHEMISTRY
COMPLEX VARIABLES	PHYSICS
DIFFERENTIAL EQUATIONS	PRE-CALCULUS
ECONOMICS	PROBABILITY
ELECTRICAL MACHINES	PSYCHOLOGY
ELECTRIC CIRCUITS	STATISTICS
ELECTROMAGNETICS	STRENGTH OF MATERIALS &
ELECTRONIC COMMUNICATIONS	MECHANICS OF SOLIDS
ELECTRONICS	TECHNICAL DESIGN GRAPHICS
FINITE & DISCRETE MATH	THERMODYNAMICS
FLUID MECHANICS/DYNAMICS	TOPOLOGY
GENETICS	TRANSPORT PHENOMENA
GEOMETRY	VECTOR ANALYSIS
HEAT TRANSFER	

*If you would like more information about any of these books,
complete the coupon below and return it to us or visit your local bookstore.*

RESEARCH & EDUCATION ASSOCIATION
61 Ethel Road W. • Piscataway, New Jersey 08854
Phone: (732) 819-8880   **website: www.rea.com**

Please send me more information about your Problem Solver books

Name _____

Address _____

City _____ State _____ Zip _____

Available at your local bookstore or order directly from us by sending in coupon below.

Available at your local bookstore or order directly from us by sending in coupon below.

The High School Tutors®

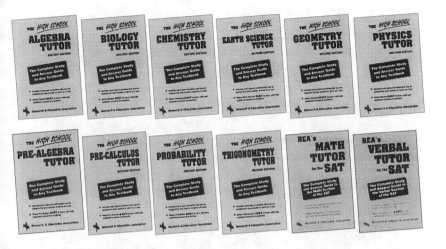

The **HIGH SCHOOL TUTOR** series is based on the same principle as the more comprehensive **PROBLEM SOLVERS**, but is specifically designed to meet the needs of high school students. REA has revised all the books in this series to include expanded review sections and new material. This makes the books even more effective in helping students to cope with these difficult high school subjects.

If you would like more information about any of these books,
complete the coupon below and return it to us or go to your local bookstore.

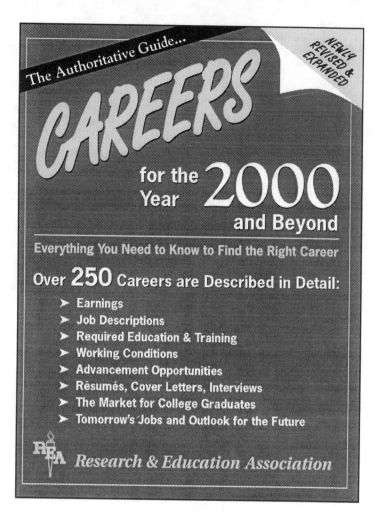